GROWING BUSINESS INNOVATION

Developing, Promoting and Protecting IP

Edited by Jonathan Reuvid

Legend Press Ltd, 107-111 Fleet Street, London, EC4A 2AB
info@legend-paperbooks.co.uk | www.legendpress.co.uk

Print: 9781789550283
Ebook: 9781789550276
Set in Times. Printing managed by Jellyfish Solutions Ltd
Cover design by Simon Levy | www.simonlevyassociates.co.uk

GROWING BUSINESS INNOVATION

DEVELOPING, PROMOTING AND PROTECTING IP

Editor: Jonathan Reuvid, Legend Business Books

Foreword   7
The Chartered Institute of Patent Attorneys

Preface   9
Jeremy Holmes, Head of IP, Imperial Innovations

List of Contributors   11

Introduction   21
The Editor

PART ONE – INNOVATION FOR TOMORROW   23

1.1 Innovation, Intention and Artificial Intelligence   25
Karren Whiteley-Brooks, Whitespace

1.2 The Innovation Conundrum – How Large Organisations Can Access Fundamental Research and Innovation   33
Mike Herd, Executive Director, Sussex Innovation

1.3 Filling the Innovation Gap between Corporates and SMEs   39
Cliff Dennett, Innovation Birmingham

1.4 Feeding China's Innovation Dragon 46
Dominic Schiller, Equipped 4 (IP) Limited / Partner Investment

1.5 Appreciative Inquiry 54
Charlie Wilson, Bosideon Consulting Ltd

PART TWO – INNOVATION FOR TOMORROW 61

2.1 Options for Brand Protection and Dispute Resolution 63
Gregor Kleinknecht, Hunters

2.2 Trolls… real or are they just in fairy tales? 70
Melanie Mode, Miller Insurance Services LLP

2.3 Protecting Against IP Disputes 76
Melanie Mode, Miller Insurance Services LLP

2.4 R&D Tax Credit Claims – an Overview of the SME 81
and Large/RDEC Schemes
Dr. Mark Graves and Julia May, May Figures Ltd

2.5 The Operation of the UK Patent Box 89
Graham Samuel-Gibbon, Taylor Wessing LLP

2.6 R&D Tax Credits – Totally Brilliant – but Not Just 95
a Walk in the Park
Terry Toms, RandD Tax

PART THREE – EXPLOITING IP OPPORTUNITIES 103

3.1 New Trends in the IP Industry 105
Christian Bunke and Natalia Korek, Basck

3.2 Patents are Not for Protecting Innovation: they are 112
for doing business
Michael Murray, Murray International Partners

3.3 The Impact of GDPR on IP work 117
Margit Hoehne, Patentgate

3.4   **Patent Landscape Study: pharmaceutical and**   124
         engineering examples
         Steven Johnson and Vedran Biondic, J&B Partners Ltd.

3.5   **IP Considerations for IT Innovation**   132
         John Collins, Creation IP

3.6   **Start-up Business: Investing and Controlling Your IP**   140
         Leah Grant, Impetus Limited

PART FOUR –STIMULATING COMMERCIAL INNOVATION   147

4.1   **R&D Tax Credit Claim Based Short-term Bridge**   149
         Finance for High-Tec Start-ups
         Dr Mark Graves, 1851 Technology Group, and Julia May, May
         Figures Ltd

4.2   **SME: University Collaboration – A Doorway into**   156
         an Opportunity-Rich Innovation Environment
         Ian Ferris, Dr. Averil Horton and Eleftheria Ledaki, Brunel
         University London

4.3   **Cross-disciplinary Innovation through Clusters**   163
         Barbara Ghinelli, Harwell Science & Innovation Campus

4.4   **Adapting Defence Technology to Business Enterprise**   170
         Paddy Bradley, Swindon and Wiltshire Local Enterprise
         Partnership

4.5   **Business Growth through Industry-Academia**   178
         Interactions
         Dr. Brian More, Coventry University

Contributors' Contacts   188

FOREWORD

'I am the co-founder of a university spin-out, developing a new therapeutic.' 'I am the proprietor of an online store, trading across Europe.' 'I am the CTO of a manufacturing SME, forecasting sales of £5.6M in 2019.'

'So what?' I hear you ask.

'We have exclusive access to our markets, enabled by our intellectual property rights.'

Now you are listening.

Intellectual property (IP) is already pivotal to your business: whether expanding into new territories, moving into new markets or launching new products, your intellectual property rights (IPRs) must work harder for you than the IPRs of your competitors work against you. So when you are investing in your business – or seeking investment from others – you need to not only secure your IP but also leverage it to your advantage. Defend what you are doing, to maintain and grow your position. Protect what you want to do, to build a monopoly. Attack where required, to clear a path forwards. Your IPRs support your strategy and your strategy may even be founded on them. If they don't, what are they doing?

But how do you transform your innovation, whether a brand, a service or a product, into an IPR of value? And how do you profit from your IPR? This book answers not only these questions but also the questions about IPRs that you didn't even know you had to ask.

The book builds on the essential framework for the process of innovation developed in the first edition. Authoritatively and comprehensively rewritten by practitioners focussed on nurturing enterprise, your journey is guided through strategic decision-making, tactical implementations and clear practical advice.

Part One examines innovation for tomorrow, including applying artificial intelligence (AI), accelerating access to R&D and feeding

China's innovation. To be part of innovation tomorrow, you must be part of it today.

Part Two explores management of IP, from disputes to taxation, via R&D tax credits and the UK Patent Box. Make your investment in IPRs self-sustaining and profit from your IPRs.

Part Three focusses on IP opportunities: new drivers and trends, evolving landscapes and where to start for a start-up. Emerging technologies disrupt markets but even established IPRs remain just as relevant. So when you look forwards, think beyond.

Part Four stimulates mutual growth through networks and collaborations: with universities, with industry, with agile SMEs and with symbiotic partners. When speed to market is determinative but you lack the essential resources – whether finance or even ideas – join forces for a win-win.

Make more from what you have and keep more of what you have got – or your competitors will. This book tells you how.

Howard Read
European Patent Attorney and Fellow of the Chartered Institute of Patent Attorneys

PREFACE

Scarcely a day goes past when either of the words "innovation" or "entrepreneurship" don't find themselves part of a headline news article, especially in the context of spin-out or University-based research. This stems from an exponential increase in the urge for academic innovators (and by academic I mean from undergraduate to Professor) to 'make their mark' in the world of business, along with an increasing acceptance from industry that the new ideas are no longer the exclusive domain of their own R&D departments.

There is a view that these are two orthogonal environments which struggle to work well together in a seamless way; in my opinion, much of this is in fact down to perception rather than reality, and the best way to dispel this is by education and communication.

In this context, I am delighted therefore to welcome a second edition of this excellent guide which addresses not only the fast-moving technological and commercial space which 'innovation' inhabits, but also the latest developments in the supporting legal framework, namely Intellectual Property (IP).

As an IP practitioner first in industry and now in 'academia', I know only too well what a difficult path it is to get an idea to business fruition, and looking at the contents of this new edition I can see it will help disentangle the interwoven strands of technical, legal and commercial challenges.

Quite rightly, the daunting topic of AI serves as an overture to a theme-packed and yet concisely constructed symphony of highly pertinent topics, each authored by an expert in the field. Articles on topics as diverse as Trolls, Innovation in China, issues around tax credits (and of course, GDPR) rub shoulders with provocative titles on what patents are really for, and how best to manage them.

I believe passionately in the need to educate everyone who is a part of this exciting entrepreneurship ecosystem in the multifarious aspects that are essential to their progress, and this guide serves as an excellent starter in that direction.

Jeremy Holmes, Head of IP
Imperial Innovations

LIST OF CONTRIBUTORS

Karren Brooks founded Whitespace at the request of her successful client base from the London Leadership Centre. She is passionate about global consciousness and the neurosciences, which help explain the emotional and mental performance required for the attainment of success and happiness. Karren is an innovative media entrepreneur and brings that valuable experience to her advisory services for business, legacy families and elite sports, organisations and athletes. She is known for her provocative interviews and remarkable breakthrough results with her clients. Karren's latest book is *Spiritual Currency – Life's Capital*.

Paddy Bradley is Director of the Swindon and Wiltshire Local Enterprise Partnership and has overall responsibility for the day-to-day running of the partnership and its operations. A highly experienced local government director, Paddy was previously Head of Economy, Skills and Property Development at Swindon Borough Council. In that role, he regularly provided strategic and operational support to SWLEP. Paddy has a wide range of experience in the public and private sectors, working as a business analyst and system adviser. He also spent 20 years in education as a teacher, headteacher and education inspector.

Christian Bunke has worked with IP for more than 20 years across many areas of technology. He has an MBA from the University of Cambridge and has built businesses and commercialised new technology through a number of start-ups. His IP experience stems from working as a patent attorney in Sweden with patent prosecution, litigation and IP strategy and includes commercialising disruptive innovation. Christian is a European Trade Mark and Design Attorney and holds a Mechanical Engineering Degree from the University of South Australia.

The Chartered Institute of Patent Attorneys (CIPA) is the professional and examining body for patent attorneys to the UK, representing virtually all the 2,000+ registered patent attorneys in the UK, whether in industry or private practice. Total membership is around 4,000 and includes judges, trainee patent attorneys and other professionals with an interest in intellectual property (patents, trade marks, designs and copyright). CIPA represents the views of professionals to policy makers at national, European and international level, with representatives sitting on a range of influential policy bodies and working groups in the UK and overseas.

Dr John Collins is European Patent and Trademark Attorney for Creation IP Limited. His expertise lies in electronics and particularly in the field of software and business method patents both in Europe and in the UK. He is a member of the Chartered Institute of Patent Attorneys (CIPA) Technology Committee and a member of the AIPL Electronics and Computer Law Committee. John has an honours degree in Medical Physics and a doctorate in Physics from London University. During his practice over more than 25 years he has acted for many different clients on a wide spectrum of matters, including prosecuting and managing extensive patent portfolios for corporations, and guiding and assisting start-up companies.

Cliff Dennett's experience in strategy, innovation and sales for companies like Orange, EDS and AT&T, combined with his start-up experience, offer a valuable skill set for creating innovation-based commercial value. His current role as Head of Commercial for Innovation Birmingham places him right at the centre of the UK's digital innovation community. Cliff grew his own technology company, securing a number of significant deals across the music and games industries and has created innovative strategies and closed numerous strategic contracts across many different industries. He has an MBA from London Business School, a BA (Hons) in International Business and a PGC in Executive Coaching.

Ian Ferris is Innovation Director, Co-Innovative Programme, Brunel University, London. As a product development specialist and innovation coach, his career spans a variety of sectors and organisations. An award-winning designer, Ian has helped create commercially successful products and services in industries spanning mid-tech, automotive, bio-materials and telecoms. As a design-led innovation coach, he has supported the technology commercialization groups in UK universities including: UCL, Oxford, Aberdeen, Bristol, Leeds, Ulster and UEA.

Ian is Innovation Director on the Brunel-EU co-funded innovation support programme Co-Innovate, where he helps SME clients grow their business though innovation.

Dr Barbara Ghinelli is Harwell Campus Business Development Director, STFC. Barbara oversees the development and management of clusters on the Harwell and Daresbury Campuses. She has established a high profile for the Space and the Health Tec Clusters and is leading the development of new Clusters including Energy Tec. Barbara joined STFC in 2010 as Executive Director of Business Development. Successes included the creation of ISIC (now Satellite Application Catapult) at Harwell and of the High Performance Computing Centre (Hartree) at Daresbury. Previously, she worked at EA (now Airbus DS) where she managed business development across Europe for the €3.2 billion joint ESA/EU Earth Observation Programme for Global Monitoring of Environment and Security (now Copernicus) and secured a number of large contracts. She graduated in Electronic Engineering at the University of York, completed her PhD in Artificial Intelligence and Radar Imaging at the University of Sheffield and holds a Certificate in Management from the Open University.

Leah Grant is Assistant Managing Director at Impetus. She has worked in Intellectual Property since she was 16 years old, initially part-time while studying for her A-Levels. During her gap year between school and university she continued to work for Impetus IP, adding to her growing expertise in all aspects of IP formalities, data management and portfolio management. After graduating from Plymouth University with a first-class honours degree in Business Management with Project Management, Leah moved to the north-west of England on secondment to work in-house for a rapidly expanding start-up business, building on her IP portfolio management skills. Today, she assists in the running of the business and has direct responsibility for major clients operating in various industries. Leah also has an in-depth knowledge of several proprietary IP management systems and has worked on data migrations and implementations. Young and fresh to the IP industry, Leah brings her skills and a new approach to the business.

Dr. Mark Graves gained a first-class MEng degree in Electronic and Structural Materials Engineering from Oxford University, where he won the Maurice Lubbock prize in the final year examinations, and a PhD in Computer Science from the University of Wales, Cardiff, winning a Royal Commission 1851 Industrial Fellowship. Mark spent 20 years running engineering and software development projects with teams in Europe, the USA and India in fields ranging from food manufacturing control to wireless sensor networks. He is the named inventor of 4 granted patents, has published 10 academic papers and book chapters in the field of machine vision and is co-editor of the book 'Machine Vision for Inspection of Natural Products.' Mark moved into the R&D Tax Credit and Patent Advisory field in 2010 and has since prepared over 700 technical claim reports in technologies ranging from software/IT, electronics and mechanical engineering through to food production and beauty products. He is a part-qualified patent attorney, having completed a post-graduate certificate in Intellectual Property Law from Bournemouth University and qualified as a Certified Patent Valuation Analyst, and has advised on and written patents for many companies including leading x-ray engineering and medical device patents. Mark is an active investor himself in early stage technology companies having shareholdings in more than 25.

Mike Herd has been Executive Director of Sussex Innovation, a business incubation network owned by the University of Sussex, since 1997. In this role, he advises commercialisation efforts that grow out of academic projects at the university, selects and advises start-ups as members of the innovation network and builds connections between public, private, academic and start-up communities. Mike has been named Sussex Businessman of the Year, won the National Achievement in Business Incubation Award and received the Queen's Award for Enterprise Promotion in recognition of his ongoing efforts to foster, promote and support entrepreneurship.

Margit Hoehne is CEO of patentGate GmbH since 2008. She has 20 years' experience with patent information, starting as a research assistant at PATON, the patent information centre in Ilmenau, Germany. Since then she has specialised in developing solutions for in-house patent monitoring workflows. Margit has a degree in business and computer science from the Technical University Ilmenau.

Dr. Averil Horton is Head of Business Development and Innovation, Brunel University, London. After a PhD in Chemistry from Imperial College she began her career as a bench chemist, later working in marketing and strategy roles for international companies. In 1997 Averil launched the futures consultancy Alpha to Omega and then in 2001 took time out to live the simple life in rural Italy, learning Italian, Visual Basic and how to cook pasta. She now specializes in the commercialisation of Intellectual Property. She earlier set up and ran the commercialization office at the National Physical Laboratory and now manages commercialisation for Brunel University.

Steven Johnson and Vedran Biondic are the founding directors of J&B Partners Ltd. and have over 20 years of searching experience between them. With degrees from Oxford University, Queen Mary, University of London and Zagreb University, they hold a wealth of technical knowledge in the areas of Chemistry, Life Sciences and Mechanical, Electrical and Aerospace Engineering. After working for larger independent search companies, J&B Partners was set up 8 years ago to provide high quality client-focused searching and IP consulting services. Working with clients large and small, they are familiar with all types of searching, with patent systems from across the globe, and using the most up-to-date databases.

Gregor Kleinknecht LLM MCIArb is a dual qualified German Rechtsanwalt and English solicitor. Following a career at large international law firms in the City of London, Gregor founded the award-winning boutique firm Klein Solicitors. He joined Hunters upon the merger of the two firms in February 2014. Gregor has a strong and broadly based contentious and non-contentious IP practice, focusing on brand protection and the exploitation, protection and enforcement of trade marks, domain names, design rights and copyright. Gregor has been recognised as the Corporate Live Wire 2014 Lawyer of the Year in the category Intellectual Property - UK.

Natalia Korek is an Intellectual Property lawyer advising clients on IP strategy, management and filing tactics. Her focus is on helping clients develop sustainable trade mark strategies in managing trade mark portfolios to maximize the value of their brand. She has extensive experience in managing trade mark portfolios in Europe and the USA, as well as across various jurisdictions in APAC. Natalia holds a Master in Laws from the University of Wroclaw.

Eleftheria Ledaki is a molecular biologist with a first class honours MSc in Molecular Basis of Human Disease from University of Crete, Greece. She has worked as a scholar in acclaimed research laboratories worldwide, with scientific findings in colon, breast cancer and DNA damage and repair. After her post-graduate studies, she worked in UCL as an honorary researcher while educating herself in Intellectual Property at Brunel University where she is a Life/Arc UTM Technology Training Fellow and works as a commercialization assistant.

Julia May is a prize-winning Chartered Accountant and Chartered Tax Advisor, formerly an Arthur Andersen corporation tax specialist. She has a BEng Honours Degree in Engineering Science from the University of Liverpool, specializing in electrical, nuclear and mechanical engineering, and broad based industry experience working for a number of software and IT consultancy firms before moving into the R&D Tax Credit field. One of the UK's leading R&D Tax Credit tax advisors, a delegate of the HMRC's Research & Development Consultative Committee and a member of the HMTC i-File Working Party, Julia has personally prepared and reviewed hundreds of R&D tax credit and, more recently, Patent Box claims. Specialising in handling HMRC inquiries on issues ranging from complications over offshore shareholder structures and taxation of capitalisation of intangible assets to basics such as inadequate record-keeping, Julia offers financial, tax modelling, fundraising and EIS or SEIS investment advice to a number of early stage technology companies where she is able to provide clients and their accountants with pragmatic commercial advice when faced with multiple interactive issues, always prioritising the overall needs of the business holistically.

Melanie Mode joined Miller Insurance Services LLP in 2004. She began her insurance career in 1997 with Helix UK Limited before moving to Clayton Risk Financing Services in 2001. Melanie specialises in assisting small and medium sized firms from all sectors who hold Intellectual Property Rights (including patents, trademarks, designs, copyrights, trade secrets and domain names), identifying the risks they may face and endeavouring to mitigate these through IP insurance. She arranges insurance cover for the defence and pursuit of IP infringement claims which include legal costs, damages, settlements and counterclaims, as well as disputes arising out of contractual obligations.

Dr. Brian More works as Director for Intellectual Property Commercialisation at Coventry University with responsibility for policy, protection, valuation and commercialisation of all forms of IP. He manages a portfolio of 20 patent families, 22 trademarks, designs and copyright. He has had 40 years' experience working with Intellectual Property, as inventor on 6 patents and jointly owned 4 trademarks. Brian has been active in starting 18 companies, using IP and attracting investment in them. Brian studied for a PhD in Grenoble as an employee of the CEA and subsequently worked at the NPL and BNFL's Company Research Laboratory. Prior to joining Coventry University, he worked as Business Development Manager for the School of Physics and Astronomy at the University of Birmingham.

He is a Director of 4 companies and sits on 3 national advisory panels. Brian has worked for private contractors on assessment of development proposals in the field of nanotechnology and on EU Framework projects as commercialisation consultant. He has an MBA in Technology Transfer and Innovation from Coventry University and was awarded the 2009 Lord Stafford Award for Technology Transfer.

Dr Michael Murray is Principal of Murray International Partners. He is a creative and scientifically literate deal-maker and negotiator with board-level experience who has led and closed a broad range of deals in the drug industry (NCEs, biologics, devices, diagnostics). Michael's experience includes divesting, acquiring, licensing-in and licensing-out of assets as well as negotiating collaborations, litigation management and resolution by negotiated settlement. He has a track record of managing and completing complex transactions, based on international networks built over a career of working in business development and licensing and commercial consultancy. Working with organisations in the US, Europe and Asia (Japan, China and Korea), Australia and New Zealand, Michael brings a deep understanding of commercialization enriched by exposure to non-pharma arenas and a strong working knowledge of intellectual property, its valuation and its use for both value creation and deal delivery.

Howard Read is a Chartered Patent Attorney and a European Patent Attorney. He is particularly keen on understanding how developments in legislation and case law impact businesses. Howard regularly represents in person before the European Patent Office, supporting Applicants, Proprietors and Opponents. As well as a BA (Hons) and MA in Natural Sciences, Howard also has a PhD in metallurgy from the University of Cambridge. In addition, he has an MSc in Computing and an LLM in Intellectual Property Law. Having worked extensively in industry on new products and in the academic sector before joining the patent profession, Howard understands the opportunities for – and the challenges to – growth. He not only appreciates the value derivable from intellectual property but also the cost due to the intellectual property of others. He very much regards intellectual property as a business tool to achieve business objectives. Howard is fluent in both English and Portuguese, has published a number of articles in scientific journals and been named as inventor on several patents.

Jonathan Reuvid is an editor and author of business books and a partner in Legend Business. He has edited all eight editions of 'The Investors' Guide to the United Kingdom' and has more than 80 editions of over 30 titles to his name as editor and part-author including 'The Handbook of International Trade', 'The Handbook of World Trade', 'Managing Cybersecurity Risk' and business guides to China, the 10 countries that joined the EU in 2004, South Africa and Morocco. Before taking up a second career in business publishing Jonathan was Director of European Operations of the manufacturing subsidiaries of a Fortune 500 multinational. From 1984 to 2005 he engaged in joint venture development and start-ups in China. He is also a founder director of IPR Events, the quality exhibition organizer and President of the charity, Community First Oxfordshire.

Graham Samuel-Gibbon is a partner in the Tax and Incentives team at Taylor Wessing LLP, a leading international law firm that advises businesses throughout their life cycle and specializes in technology, media and communications, life sciences and private wealth. Graham is a highly experienced tax specialist with an extensive track record in advising a wide range of UK and foreign-based companies, from start-ups to FTSE 100 and Fortune 500 multinational groups, on a broad range of advisory and transactional tax matters, with a particular focus on tax issues relating to the development, ownership and exploitation of IP rights.

Dominic Schiller is a practicing UK and European Patent and Trademark Attorney with over 30 years' experience. He has a Master's in Business Administration and works closely with corporate finance organizations, technology due diligence experts and business incubators and accelerators in the UK and China. He founded his own patent and trademark firm Equipped 4 (IP) Limited and is an investor, and the in-house adviser, to several IP rich technology companies, operating across a diverse range of industries including manufacturing, healthcare, pharmaceuticals and the creative industries. He has managed international collaborations, licensing and Joint Ventures with both large and small entities.

Dominic also runs Partner Investment with Ning Qu, a leading medical doctor and Professor with positions in the Netherlands and China. Partner Investment provides Technology Transfer support services between China, Europe and Australia and is working on creating a China/Europe/Australia investment fund to support their exiting cross-country activities.

Terry Toms is Managing Director of RandDTax which provides consultancy services and scopes projects to assess R&D Tax Credit claims, working mainly with innovative SME, accountancy practices and trade bodies. The RandDTax team of UK experts offer an unrivalled service through a hands-on approach, specialist tax and technical knowledge and a strong relationship with HMRC. This award-winning formula is used on a daily basis to identify R&D Tax Credit eligibility for UK businesses across a broad range of industry sectors.

Charlie Wilson OBE is a coach who specialises in team working and leadership under pressure. Executives come to him when they want to develop the disciplines they need for consistent performance in challenging conditions. His first career was in the Royal Navy in which he was a successful leader in a wide range of situations and an integral member of a variety of high-performing teams.

INTRODUCTION

This second edition of *Growing Business Innovation* takes readers further into exploring the nature of innovation, its essential role in the profitable development of business enterprises, its close relationship with intellectual property (IP) and the role of academia in its stimulation.

The contents are arranged in four parts, with the first section looking ahead at new challenges for innovation, already apparent, including artificial intelligence (AI), China's growing activity in innovative development and appreciative inquiry. Part Two revisits the management of IP with new chapters on security threats, protection and dispute resolution together with authoritative overviews by leading practitioners of R&D tax credits, how to access them and the operation of the UK patent box.

In the third part opportunities for the exploitation of IP are discussed against the impact of threats from GDPR and emerging technologies. The final section of the book identifies the benefits for SMEs from working with universities and research institutes, explains the use of R&D tax credit claims to generate short-term bridging loans for start-ups and cites examples of harnessing defence technology for commercial innovation.

As usual, I am indebted to all authors for their insightful views and informative texts and to their firms for their essential advertising support. Our thanks also to Howard Read for his foreword on behalf of the Chartered Institute of Patent Attorneys and to Peter Holmes of Imperial Innovations for his Preface. The contact details of all authors are listed in Appendix and readers seeking further advice on their topics are encouraged to be in direct touch.

Jonathan Reuvid
Editor

PART ONE
INNOVATION FOR TOMORROW

1.1
INNOVATION, INTENTION AND ARTIFICIAL INTELLIGENCE

Karren Whitely-Brooks Whitespace

While many of the chapters in this edition deal with specific details about Intellectual Property and the financial and tax implications of funding and protecting inventors, this opening chapter will deal with the more fundamental questions of the innovative process. The questions discussed will include, why a business should innovate? And how to make wise choices using the latest technological advances in artificial intelligence?

WHY INNOVATE? WHAT DOES IT REALLY MEAN?

If you take as a given that innovation is necessary for any business, and indeed society, to advance and flourish; then you may be reading this book to find an edge in your quest to improve your company. If however, you are an inventor, then you may ***not*** have the requisite mindset to be an innovator. Common wisdom would argue that if one can invent something then, surely, one is automatically, an innovator. The confusion begins when one reviews the popular definitions for the noun, innovation. Merriam-Webster Dictionary offers these definitions: ***1. The introduction of something new.*** And goes on to state in its second most common definition: ***2. A new method, idea or device.***
When one explores other knowledge sources such as Wikipedia, they begin with the same definition for innovation as "*something*

new" but go on to expand the idea by stating, "*innovation takes place through the provision of more-effective products, processes... that are made available to markets, governments and society*". If however, the inventor, who builds a *better* mousetrap, does not require a-*brand new*-mousetrap and the inventor is able to commercialise and positively affect society with his mousetrap, then that inventor is truly an innovator. Innovations are thus, incremental improvements which satisfy our clients' needs and demands rather than just something new or different.

The futurist and author, Jacob Morgan gives a more easily understood example, which is important if you and your company want to innovate. He asks, "Is Google Glass an invention or an innovation?", and offers in contrast, "Is the Apple iPhone an innovation or an invention?". This is not just a discussion of semantics but goes to the core of the dilemma. If the invention of Google Glass, while novel and definitionally appearing to be an innovation, remains an oddity with little commercial acceptance or demand; then the invention of Google Glass, he argues, is *not* an innovation. The iPhone, Morgan states, is "both new and has had a profound influence in the way we communicate, store and access data" which makes it truly an innovation. It is as Wikipedia offers, "the more-effective" inventions which result in an innovation and the inventor and his company, to be classified as an innovator.

At a recent social gathering, I was asked, "what are you working on?" and I replied," we are helping a business foment innovation." My friend immediately asked, "what have they invented?" My reply was, "they have invented a new **intention**, and indeed, a new **mindset**." I wasn't being glib or enigmatic but have found that the stated intention to innovate, which includes the goal of delivering something new or at least better and the mindset to commercialise the output of their work, are the two basic requisites for any company to be considered, truly innovative.

'INTENTIONS HAVE NO INTELLIGENCE'

Unfortunately, the word *new* and the promise of innovation have become ubiquitous in our lives, as any visit to the supermarket will attest. It is obvious in every aisle of our shopping that *new* and *improved* can apply to everything from apples to zucchinis. All too often, leaders of business have a mindset which says, 'innovation is just some business school hype or marketing speak.' The scepticism surrounding innovation is that it has little relevance to the day-to-day operation of the company. We strongly suggest the company "vision" or "mission statement" which is necessarily a broad generalisation to be delivered over a long period, should include the ***intelligent intention*** to innovate. The company's long view must be accompanied by the short-term deliverable projects, which will become commercially viable and make a difference to our clients and shareholders.

The following diagram demonstrates how the importance of long and short-term goals relate to a company's ability to innovate. We would argue that in all three areas of Mission, Strategic Goals and Operating Objectives there must be a stated and determined intention to innovate; not lip service, but a firm and communicated intention; not just a hope but an intelligent intention.

The requirement for specific and short-term projects to produce commercial success is the test, which will prove whether the new product or process is truly innovative.

Figure 1.1.1 – Time horizons for short and long term goals

Ever since Peter Drucker argued in the Harvard Business review in 1996 that "Innovation is the specific function of entrepreneurship", business consultancies have been attempting to assist companies to change their mindset. Drucker's premise instructs companies to promote "wealth producing resources" as a fundamental goal for their employees. As the twenty-first century continues to make great advances in Artificial Intelligence, it appears that business leaders may now be hoping that technology will provide these much sought after resources and innovations.

WILL ARTIFICIAL INTELLIGENCE ASSIST INNOVATION?

Arvind Krishna, Director of IBM Research says, "Faced with a constant onslaught of data, we needed a new type of system that learns and adapts and we now have that with AI". Krishna further states, regarding the use of AI in business innovation, "What was deemed impossible a few years ago is not only becoming possible, it's very quickly becoming necessary and expected".

In just the last decade AI has exploded because of the combination of big data with powerful graphics processing units (GPUs), which has benefited from employing the well-known model of Deep Learning. We all remember the stories of Deep Blue which was programmed by the forefathers of IBM Research back in the 20th century and which culminated in a competition with the Russian Chess Master, Gary Kasparov in 1996. It was IBM's Deep Learning which allowed the computer to analyse the millions of chess moves and which revealed Artificial Intelligence as one of the most important technologies to be developed in the 21st century.

It is this Deep Learning popularised by Deep Blue, which will be educated by Deep Reasoning in order to create a new technology, enabling machines to conduct unsupervised learning. It is the human brain function of unsupervised learning, which continues to baffle the technologists. IBM Research is attempting to make machines curious and to seek answers. These machines will indeed produce new questions, as they learn from each other, but this is proving far more difficult than the much discussed language and image recognition applications.

The emotional side of facial recognition, for example, and the reasoning which humans develop from a young age, is much more difficult for Deep Learning to grasp. Computer scientists are working with neuroscientists and psychiatrists to help the advanced computer facial recognition of emotional indications. Dr. Fei Fei, Professor of Computer Science at Stanford University, says AI image recognition, struggles to identify and interpret emotions; the computer's cognition is similar to the human condition classified as Alexithymia. This is a condition which inhibits some humans from both expressing and recognising emotions, often accompanying Autism and other psychological disorders. IBM research, however, has made great strides in image recognition which is helping identify and diagnose a variety of illness and pathologies.

One example of AI image recognition is the computer application which assists the clinician in recognising melanoma lesions on human skin. While a clinician may be confident in recognising a certain type of lesion within a predominant racial skin colour, they dramatically increase their diagnostic ability with the AI database. The computer is able to compare, select and identify from a much greater range of images and skin tones and alert the doctor to possible areas of concern from patients they are not accustomed to treating. The use of AI in pathological recognition and diagnosis meets the societal impact criteria for innovation.

ARTIFICIAL INTELLIGENCE AND DECISIONS

Hollywood and science fiction authors may sensationalise the possibilities for unethical or humanity-threatening decisions from Artificial Intelligence; however, most computer scientists find this dystopic vision to be less than probable. The fascination with the human brain and the sensory inputs which we take for granted, underlines the complexity and difficulty in using Artificial Intelligence to actually reason. The intersection of Deep Learning with Deep Reasoning will produce innovative products and help business leaders make better and more informed decisions.

Aya Soffer, IBM Director of AI and Cognitive Analytics Research, says "computers don't have common sense". Humans grow up "understanding gravity" and inertia and the physical properties which allow us to function. A simple example of "objects staying where they are put", or moving, if influenced by wind or vibration or gravity is extremely complex for AI to comprehend on the mathematical level. It is the human, common sense, which is a mysterious combination of learned and inherent genetic wisdom, which is difficult for the computer models to simulate and understand.

Our life experience may however, make common sense decisions difficult. One popular test of common sense, which is easily passed by 4 and 5 year olds, is almost always failed by adult participants. It starts with the simple question of, "How do you put a Giraffe in a refrigerator?". Most adults struggle, consider size and cutting up pieces etc. while the child answers "You open the door and put in the Giraffe and close the door". The test continues with, "How do you put an Elephant in the refrigerator?" adults again, consider size and possibilities, animal cruelty and many permutations, while children, who learn and remember with greater focus on short term memory, answer correctly: "You open the refrigerator and take out the Giraffe and put in the Elephant". While humorous, the quiz does illustrate how complicated and layered our decision-making process can become after years of apparently logical conclusions.

If the confluence of Deep Reasoning with Deep Learning can assist the innovator with decision making, then it stands to reason that more useful inventions and applications will be made available. If machine learning struggles with common sense and emotional components, it is important to understand the human decision making process. It is correct decision making which is critical for the creative employees and inventors to produce a viable product. Artificial intelligence is credited with the image and voice recognition which has produced innovative products like Amazon's Alexa and Apple's iPhone. The retrieval of libraries of information now resident on our smartphone is another example of machines assisting humans in decision making. The basic human cognitive function is now being studied using Quantum Theory, which will improve the Deep Reasoning technology and accelerate the human decision making process.

QUANTUM COGNITION

While computers are learning from the human capacity to increase the machine's perceptive abilities, the world of Quantum Theory is helping humans understand their own mental faculties. Artificial Intelligence can recognise faces and pathologies and can understand voice and a variety of human speech and languages, but it is the nuance of human perception which continues to be difficult. We can teach a computer to see and perceive a square but human vision can see and intuitively perceive three dimensions, as in the cube below, although it is obviously drawn in only two dimensions. Humans can see both the facial profiles, as well as the Urn, in the second image below and decide contextually which image is the more applicable. The human brain is being studied to understand what allows us to have these simultaneously efficient perceptions and intuitions.

Figure 1.1.2 – Perceptions of three dimensions

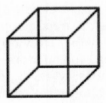

The human brain is often said to rely on intuition or "gut" reactions and this Quantum Cognition is being understood on a molecular and chemical level. The mind, however, is not the brain and the distinction is important, if innovators are to develop the correct mindset and an accurate decision making process. Daniel Siegel, UCLA psychiatrist and author, defines the mind and distinguishes it from the brain as follows: "The mind is an embodied and relational process in relationship to other minds that regulates the flow of energy and information in the whole ecosystem." He further explains, "Your mind is listening as I am sharing thoughts and those thoughts are converted into electrical impulses".

The further development of Artificial Intelligence will increasingly understand the human mind's electrical impulses and become part of, and possibly linked directly to, the mind's ecosystem. A variety of recent studies have defined these mental information flows throughout the human nervous system. So the idea of an emotionally "heavy heart" or a "gut feeling" is a scientifically correct way to map our human thought process. If you are an inventor and an aspiring innovator, the important take-away from these discoveries is that one should trust their instincts and commit to decisions. Commitment to your invention and the passion to procure the investment funding is key to the commercial success of your ideas.

DECISIONS AND CHOICES

It is clear that Deep Learning can provide the data to help test your inventive theories and that machine intelligence can be a key component of the team you assemble to produce your innovation. Different academic disciplines including psychiatry, neurobiology, psychology and even philosophy are studying how we make choices and decide. Because of the human emotional component to our thought process, the lack of emotion in deep learning and deep reasoning, provided by Artificial Intelligence, can produce more objective conclusions, untainted by preconceived notions and human foibles. The importance of choice has been studied for thousands of years and the mathematician and discoverer of the geometrical theorem which carries his name said:

"Choices are the hinges of destiny." - *Pythagoras (570 BC - 495 BC), Greek philosopher*

If your destiny is to be an innovator and contribute to an innovative enterprise then your decision-making and the choices required will be fundamental to your success. We are often asked for an easy process to increase one's probability of reaching the correct conclusion. Artificial Intelligence can help in the information and analysis of the data to form an informed decision. Seeking the programmes which can test your theories in a time and economically efficient manner will help your project realise its objective. Our Whitespace team offers this innovative process, which describes the important components, leading to inspired decisions...

Whitespace consultancy has coined the acronym **RED-OP** to assist with your important decisions:

R. *retrieve* all the data and pertinent information available (Artificial Intelligence will help).

E. *evaluate* the factors and outcomes (AI can test your probable outcomes).

D. *deliberate* and follow your intuition, your heart and indeed your gut.

O. *opt* for the best solution by the deadline which you have set. Time is definitely money.

P. *passionately commit* to your decision and communicate your firm intention to your team.

EXECUTIVE SUMMARY AND CONCLUSION

The definition of innovation must include the commercial viability of the product, process, or service; just being new, or better, is not sufficient to achieve innovation. In order to move an idea or desire to produce an innovation, the firm intention, communicated to the entire organisation, and indeed potential clients, is a fundamental requirement for success. While the intention to innovate is often found in long-term mission statements, it is even more important in short-term, time constrained, projects.

Artificial Intelligence can be an important contributor to the innovative process. AI will complement, supplement and verify the human's decisions and choices. The inventor must tune into and listen to the entire mind's ecosystem when making a decision. The most important element in the innovative process is one's passionate and communicated commitment. Good luck.

1.2

THE INNOVATION CONUNDRUM

How large organisations can access fundamental research and innovation

Mike Herd, Executive Director, Sussex Innovation

There is a gap in our marketplace of ideas. Innovation in business tends to be driven by the biggest and the smallest organisations; the tech behemoths at one end of the scale, and the lean start-ups at the other. In between, true innovation is often difficult to achieve.

We need a new term to describe this kind of organisation – too large to be considered SMEs, but too small to bother the FTSE 500. Hundreds of employees, turning over tens of millions, but rarely a household name. Sometimes large public-sector bodies fit the description too. Let's call them LSEs: Large, Stable Enterprises.

What these LSEs all have in common is that they've built a structure that does a specific job consistently, but one that has almost never needed to change or adapt. This could be due to a lack of challengers or disruptors in their sector, or established relationships with reliable clients who help to insulate them from failure. That's not to say that they aren't open to innovative or disruptive methods; they simply haven't been able to make them happen.

"54% of innovating companies struggle to bridge the gap between innovation strategy and business strategy." – PwC, Reinventing Innovation

Why should this be the case? Well, through no fault of their own, many organisations of this type simply fall prey to short-term thinking. The pressures of focusing on sales and customers mean that there is often an inability to step outside of the immediate challenge and look at the wider picture.

The scale of the LSE also tends to lend itself to rigid budgetary cycles, which in turn lend themselves to inflexible R&D programmes. That's fine if you want to achieve incremental innovation within strict parameters – making an existing product work better over time, for example – but it isn't going to achieve a real step change in how you do business.

Many internal innovation programmes are also hampered by how the organisation defines success. For example, is their key performance indicator customer retention, rather than opening up new markets? Do they judge 'innovation' by counting the number of patents filed, rather than how their internal process has changed?

CORPORATE ACCELERATORS AND OPEN INNOVATION NETWORKS

The current solutions adopted by most organisations in this situation are either to launch a corporate accelerator, or to set an innovation challenge through an open innovation network. Both approaches have their flaws:

Corporate Accelerators are:

- A marketplace dominated by bigger brands
- Not managed or overseen by key stakeholders within the business

Open Innovation Networks are:

- Not particularly agile
- Constrained by narrow framing of challenges

Both are:

- Inward- rather than outward-facing
- Seeking ready-made solutions, rather than delivering collaborative innovation

The corporate accelerator model involves inviting technology start-ups from the host's industry to pitch their products. From this group of start-ups, a select few are welcomed onto an accelerator programme and provided with financial support, expertise and resources to "hothouse" their development. It is often unclear whether the ultimate benefit to the business is intended to be a strategic advantage, or financial gain.

The corporate accelerator market is dominated by multinationals and bigger brands. Even if you have deep pockets, it's very difficult to garner the kind of publicity that will attract a queue of relevant start-ups without being backed by a household name.

Typically, these programmes are also completely siloed from the day-to-day operations of the business, managed by MBAs with no direct experience of the company's inner workings. This restricts the potential for collaboration and results in innovation being delivered in a prescriptive manner.

Open innovation networks can result in entrepreneurs having to operate under similar constraints. The standard model for these networks is that a problem is posed directly to the marketplace, in a similar approach to government-sponsored innovation challenges. However, where the likes of Innovate UK offer grant funding to achieve broad, society-changing goals, open innovation networks generally issue more narrow requests.

The problem is in how these challenges are framed – the organisation issuing the challenge tends to approach it with the same inward-facing mindset that hampers most internal R&D efforts. A simple example of this is the way the challenge is often phrased: "Company X has a requirement for product Y" rather than "Company X is trying to address problem Z". These kinds of narrow requests seek a specific, ready-made solution that fits within a marketplace the organisation already understands, rather than disrupting or challenging the status quo in any way.

Both these approaches can be seen as threatening the position of the LSE. A global corporate making a dramatic change to one of their products or their business model can very quickly change the whole industry supply chain, where many of the LSEs operate. On the other hand, an entrepreneurial start-up coming through an accelerator, or backed by VC funding, has a strong chance of disrupting and threatening the existing market place. Clearly, this is not necessarily the ideal model for collaboration.

AN INNOVATORS' EYE VIEW

"The need for innovation in medium to large companies has never been greater. The Business to Business market is increasingly taking the lead from the Consumer market in technological enhancement and the

pace of change ever quickens. This means that larger companies need to partner with smaller start-ups to harness specialist technologies, innovation and expertise which it would be inequitable to have in house. This allows a lean model for innovation which benefits both sides." – David Lane, Head of Technology, Arcus Holdings

From our position at Sussex Innovation, a business incubation network owned by the University of Sussex, we get to see the flaws of these structures from the perspective of the innovators themselves. We work with two kinds – academic researchers, and early-stage companies.

Within a University, most academics are trained to talk about their research in a very specific way, highlighting the process and the insights it generates. To take the output of that research to a market requires a very different skillset – it needs to be framed around the applications of the research, and the commercial implications of the insight. To put it in business terminology, there is a tendency to talk about features rather than benefits.

Start-ups, meanwhile, will usually talk about what products they have already built, rather than what they're working on. There are also challenges around implementation when an early-stage company takes its first step into the corporate world. The time frames involved can be radically different, while there are often problems with integrating a new technology into existing systems architecture and processes.

Another common frustration comes with stress testing business models designed for the SME market in a corporate environment. To give just one example, many Software as a Service (SaaS) products are built on the assumption that every purchaser will operate like the start-up business that created the product. They don't have experience of the requirements of an enterprise-level solution, or the means to manage internal compliance. There won't be an individual executive who has the single credit card that they do business with.

Of course, all of these problems are solvable, and there are many systems integration businesses that can translate their business process innovation into an enterprise solution – but most small business developers don't have those skills.

Accelerator models are usually focused on the start-up having the right entrepreneurial management team to rapidly scale the business. Such management talent is both rare and expensive, and is not commonly found in the same business as the technical or creative innovator. Understandably, Venture Capitalists also back management teams rather than focusing on ideas. The reason is that a good entrepreneur – as opposed to an inventor – is more likely to adapt, evolve and pivot an idea to meet market need.

This doesn't mean that a good idea or a novel innovation is any less good or less novel just because the inventor doesn't have the right business acumen and entrepreneurial mindset. Finding new ways to introduce new ideas into the LSE market, which is focused on delivery, can open up whole new areas of innovation and productivity growth.

THE SOLUTION: A NEW MODEL OF INNOVATION NETWORK

What the majority of LSEs need in order to break this cycle is access to a broad portfolio of innovations, curated outside of their R&D process. By creating clusters of different types of solution within this portfolio, we can start to present relevant innovation back to relevant individuals within the organisation. By working directly with a CTO, Finance Manager or HR Director, innovators can gain a much deeper understanding of the real challenges faced by the different functions of the business.

"Hyper-collaborative companies must make use of an eclectic group of partners to challenge senior management thinking and encourage a continuous process of unlearning and relearning." – Navi Radjou and Jaideep Prabhu, Frugal Innovation

Through its Business Research Academic Innovation Network (BRAIN) project[1], Sussex Innovation is making a direct intervention to help LSEs find innovation, and to help innovators find their market. There are several principles underpinning this:

- Real 'open innovation' must involve conversation and collaboration;
- It must involve a broad enough portfolio of ideas to challenge and prompt creative thought;
- LSEs need an "innovation champion" to assess ideas, prove their credibility and secure buy-in;
- The LSE should ideally act as a mentor as well as a customer in the relationship;
- Collaborations can lead to new commercial opportunities for all parties.

The model involves identifying early stage businesses and academics, who are selected on the criteria of having an innovation with potential

---

1. The BRAIN project is a Coast to Capital LEP project, part-funded by a grant from the European Regional Development Fund.

and relevance to a particular market, rather than on the past experience of their management team.

From the other side of the equation, LSE businesses and organisations are selected on the criteria of being open to talking about their needs and opportunities in their market, rather than the contents of their latest accelerator call.

In short, the project has been designed to bridge the gap between real innovation and real needs.

This often means that the solutions involved don't come ready-made, and require a "customer-mentor" relationship on the part of the LSE. Sometimes the innovation turns out to be a solution for something completely different to its original purpose.

For example, one project involved a sensor that was originally built to monitor electric potential signals for taking electrocardiogram measurements of the human heart. A completely different opportunity was also identified, in monitoring the condition of electrical appliances.

The important lesson to take from this story is that a specialist within an LSE can often spot potential applications for an innovation that are well outside of the innovator's experience. Multi-sector experience – and exposure to new sectors outside of your experience – are hugely important to helping inventions find their market opportunity.

Many new technology solutions also have the potential to create deep and lasting impact across multiple sectors. For example, new applications built upon expertise in psychology can be used to better recruit, integrate and motivate teams – a product that clearly should be relevant to any employer. Or who would know that some of the biggest markets for installing solar power systems in the UK are universities, water companies and retail sites?

1.3

FILLING THE INNOVATION GAP BETWEEN CORPORATES AND SMES

Cliff Dennett, Innovation Birmingham

Innovation is very hard. Creativity is easier but turning those ideas into sustainable products and services is much harder. Our minds work at lightning speeds; just a single mind can easily create thousands of ideas in a single day (you need to keep the coffee on, clear your day and buy a lot of sticky notes) but when it comes to turning those ideas into businesses, that mind needs to engage with other minds and that's where the challenges start.

Minds inside large organisations have different world views to those inside start-up businesses. The vocabulary, corporate culture and ability to operate is very different to that in an early-stage business. Corporates have decision-hierarchies, rigid budget processes and employee reward mechanisms that can sit completely at odds with the flatter structures, flexible strategy and founder motivations of the start-up.

For smaller companies, speed is everything. It doesn't really have anything to do with enthusiasm or energy; there are plenty of corporate employees who can equal the verve and drive of the archetypal entrepreneur. Speed is a necessity for smaller companies because they are invariably always about to run out of money. To book a meeting in the calendars of most budget-holding, decision-wielding senior managers in large corporates might take three months. That's a single quarter for a corporate and a lifetime for most early stage businesses. If those businesses are lucky enough to have secured some early stage funding, it may give them a single year's runway at best, so waiting for a quarter of that time is tough (and stressful).

People in large companies love talking to people in smaller companies because the latter are usually perceived as doing something new, cool and exciting. Often the more senior people (those that can make the decisions and spend the money) have been in that company, or another of similar size and type, for many years and so relish looking at the new. This is fine, if there is a mechanism for turning that conversation into commercial benefit for both parties. All too often though, SME-corporate engagements suck up everyone's time for little gain. For the corporate employee, all that's happened are a few welcome and interesting meetings to break up the days' usual pressures but for the start-up business, such time-drains can be fatal.

Despite the call for innovation and the worry of market disruption threatening obsolescence to incumbent businesses, employee reward structures generally are not set up to encourage innovation. Most large companies have become big because they have developed a competence at a particular product, service or operation. Business planning and management processes are established to try and maintain and improve that competence and so anything new and radical has a hard time getting air time at the right meetings.

This leads to corporate employees becoming inherently risk averse; they have to be, in order to deliver against the company's core competence and therefore to protect their monthly salaries, bonuses and pension contributions. Corporate employees gain and secure these things by being risk averse and start-up founders gain these things by taking calculated risks. While the emotional drive is there to cooperate, the practical realities of paying mortgages often gets in the way.

In practical terms, this can often lead to mis-aligned meetings and expectations. The excitement of securing a meeting with a large established brand can feel very exciting for the SME. Even an early meeting starts appearing on investor reports and often unrealistic expectations are placed on these early encounters. This in turn puts pressure on the SME's founder to deliver; to "get the deal done". While most seasoned investors appreciate the fragility of these early meetings, the growth in tax incentives such as EIS and SEIS in the UK have led to a significant growth in the number of new investors; people who are often making their first investment and may have unrealistic expectations of how fast a large company may commit to working with a SME.

LARGE FIRM – SMALL FIRM INTERACTION

I've seen the dynamic of large firm-small firm interaction play out many times. The founder may meet a corporate contact at a business event, exchanging cards with the promise of a meeting. The SME will put the contact on their prospects list and make the first follow up calls or emails. After two-three attempts, the contact may respond, often asking for more information; "Send us your pitch/slide deck/ brochure/1-pager". The corporate contact is probably genuinely personally interested and wants to 'help'. After two-three months, the first meeting may finally happen; perhaps the corporate contact has convened some of their colleagues, all of whom will likely be interested in the new gizmo being offered. At the end of the meeting, a follow up meeting may be offered but only after the start-up founder has jumped through a couple of hoops; "Can you mock this up in our brand style?" or "What would this look like with [X] functionality?" and so continues the dance until the corporate employee changes job, loses budget, the start up goes bust or the contact just dries up.

This brief and rather cynical account describes the misalignment between small and large firms of what academic researchers Cohen and Levinthal termed 'absorptive capacity'[2]; a firm's "ability to recognize the value of new information, assimilate it, and apply it to commercial ends." Many large companies just have no idea how to integrate the offering of a SME, despite the positive intentions of those involved. Many SMEs have had little experience of the decision-making processes and timescales of large companies, so expect everything to be done in days or weeks rather than months and years.

Furthermore, perhaps unsurprisingly, Cohen and Levinthal suggest that a large firm generates a greater understanding (and presumably commercial return) from engaging in external innovation, the more they do it. There is no universal 'playbook' when it comes to securing innovation from external sources. Large firms need to commit and invest in external innovation and learn how their particular company culture and business model can absorb the new, turning it into competitive advantage. This takes time, focus, the right people and, most importantly, belief.

Large firms can gain access to innovation by engaging in structured innovation activities that connect these large firms in the right ways with SMEs.

---

2. Cohen and Levinthal (1990), "Absorptive capacity: A new perspective on learning and innovation", Administrative Science Quarterly, Volume 35, Issue 1 pg. 128-152

THE SERENDIP® PROGRAMME

The Serendip® programme at Innovation Birmingham brings together corporate partners and SMEs into facilitated networks of exchange, helping SMEs engage with large firms and those large firms to contract with new innovations relevant to their core business. Serendip® co-locates corporate partners together with cohorts of SMEs, encouraging collaboration across corporates as well as between SMEs and corporates.

The programme has been running since 2015 and has already produced many successful outcomes for both small and large firms, including;

- Small firm [A] created a platform that connects multi-property landlords with tenants, handling communication flows, certification, maintenance etc. Large firm [B] operates in the financial services industry and is licensing firm A's platform technology as a new white-label solution for its clients.
- Large firm [C] is a significant public sector transport operator looking for new innovation to increase organisational efficiencies. Small firm [D] created an app to notify the hard of hearing when an alarm sounded, doorbell rang etc. D's service captures the audio fingerprint of sounds – a little like Shazam but for sound effects. The two companies are now creating early warning systems that listen to mechanical devices and that will alert people when mechanical components are going 'off tune', so indicating early signs of impending failure – a b2b process efficiency born from a b2c consumer proposition.
- Small firm [E]'s artificial intelligence health platform allows health data to be turned into actionable insights. Public health provider [F] is rolling this out across a number of hospitals to help save the £millions lost per year in staff sickness.

To make a programme like Serendip® work and to help cost such an activity, here are the key cornerstones that need to be put in place to make an innovation activity work for your company:

1. **A multi-year (at least 3-5 year) commitment**. This is more important, the earlier the better for the large firm in its innovation journey. There are three primary reasons for this:
    (i)   The large firm needs to learn how to internalise innovations from SMEs. At the start, internal resistance may be robust against the new for the reasons already

outlined and large firms need to learn the internal processes and relationships needed to realise value out of engaging with SMEs;

(ii)   The firm needs to send a clear signal to the rest of the organisation that it is serious about innovation and that the initiative is not just a fad;

(iii)   Depending on the stage of innovation and SME, it usually takes a good eighteen months - two years for a SME's innovation to start making traction within a large firm and three months to run a promotion, assessment and induction process to find, recruit and engage a sufficient volume of high quality SMEs. As the programme becomes established and all parties learn how to internalise innovation, these timescales will shrink.

2.   **In the right place**. We have found the best way to do this is by establishing the innovation activity on 'neutral ground', offsite from core operations but not too distant for it to feel disconnected. This also allows the involvement of other corporate and supply chain partners. It helps greatly if the location sits with other innovation activity and other knowledge-intensive businesses. Being nearby to universities helps as does being located in or very near to city centres, creating the right kind of energy, flow of talent and events activity. You can probably budget for around 200-300 sq ft of workspace per early stage business, depending of course on their company size. Most of the businesses on the Serendip® programme at Innovation Birmingham are between 2-5 people with a few having 10-15.

3.   **With the right people**. Having the right people onsite at the innovation facility is vital. Externalised innovation facilities have received criticism in the past as being vanity projects with those working in them being seen as aloof, or disconnected from the core business, receiving special treatment, or 'easy' jobs. We have found that an innovation facility nurturing 20-30 SMEs per year benefits from 1-3 staff allocated to the innovation programme. These staff should be superb sign-posters, ideally with experience across multiple functions in the core business. They will have built up a great network across their company and therefore significant social capital upon which to draw. With 'insider knowledge',

they will also help the SME entrepreneurs build a much more relevant business case for the large firm to adopt their innovation. They'll probably spend 3/5ths of their time onsite at the innovation facility and 2/5ths networking back into the core operations. These people will be complemented by staff at the innovation facility. Your company staff will provide the domain-specific knowledge and important connectivity back into the core operation. The staff at the facility will conduct the programme admin, help in PR, marketing and recruitment, recording value created and arrange mentoring, expert sessions and events.

4. **Active events programme**. If you engage with an innovation service provider, they can help with this. No SME is an island and creating a vibrant social and business events programme helps facilitate those important connections back into the core operation, the supply chain and other potential external partners. It also creates that all important sense of community, providing the more informal and ad-hoc support that SMEs need.

5. **Set challenges but remain open**. All of the corporate partners on Serendip® have set market-based challenges which they are looking to the SME community to help resolve. Usually, the corporate will set 4-6 of these, revising them every two years. SMEs are asked to respond to these during the application process, describing how their technology addresses the challenge. We also have a wildcard option where SMEs can submit applications that they feel might still be relevant even though they don't specifically address one of the challenges. About half of those accepted onto the programme are responding to one of the 4-6 challenges and about half are accepted due to some left-field thought the SME has had about how its technology can help the corporate. This is another key benefit of innovation programmes; often, we don't know what we don't know until someone else tells us. Our own myopia caused by years of operating in the same industry can cause us to become blinkered by the dominant logic of that industry. SMEs can really help break that.

6. **Measures**: It is impossible to predict if and when a particular innovation will appear of course, but outputs can be set to encourage this to happen ... number of new SMEs accepted onto the programme every year (of course passing quality

thresholds), number of trials completed, deals signed, innovations integrated etc. Particularly with digital innovations the impact can be so vast that a 5 year programme, nurturing 50 businesses, producing just a couple of innovations adopted by the organisation can make a significant difference to that firm's bottom line.

CONCLUSION

Internalising innovation from external sources is always going to be challenging but it can create significant economic advantage for those companies willing to invest in innovation for the long term. It can take 1-2 years to establish a robust innovation activity that is properly connected into the core business but once established, with a sustained focus, the returns can be significant. Culturally, bringing SMEs into a large firm over time can help the larger company become more agile and think differently while still retaining its core competencies and therefore be particularly relevant in industries that are undergoing significant structural shifts. As digital connectivity continues to flip the business models of many industries, gaining access to innovation will become increasingly vital to the future success of many large companies. It's too risky not to do it.

1.4

FEEDING CHINA'S INNOVATION DRAGON

Dominic Schiller, Equipped 4 (IP) Limited / Partner Investment

In real estate we often hear that the key to a successful investment is: "Location, Location, Location". Similarly, profiting from innovation is all about exploiting and commercialising your Intellectual Property Rights.

As Intellectual Property Rights are territorial in nature, knowing what rights are available in China and understanding their relative strengths and weaknesses compared to other major territories, are fundamental to being able to answer the question:

"Is it safe to feed China's innovation dragon, and if so, how do we go about it?"

This article seeks to provide the reader with a background to China's changing landscape with regards to:

- Innovation;
- Intellectual Property Rights; and
- Technology Transfer

in order that they can make an informed decision on whether to look to the Chinese market, and if they conclude that they want to access it, how they might do so, as safely and effectively as possible.

There is no doubt that historically many UK companies with Intellectual Property Rights have dismissed the Chinese market, primarily due to difficulties in accessing this market and concerns over intellectual property theft, focusing instead on local markets, such as Europe and the United States. I would suggest that this paradigm is now outdated and that the new watchword for any company, particularly a technology start-up, is: ignore the potential of China at your peril.

Why is this? One striking visual that emphasises the significance of Innovation and the Chinese market is illustrated in the Figure 1.4.1 below:

Figure 1.4.1 – Innovation and the Chinese market

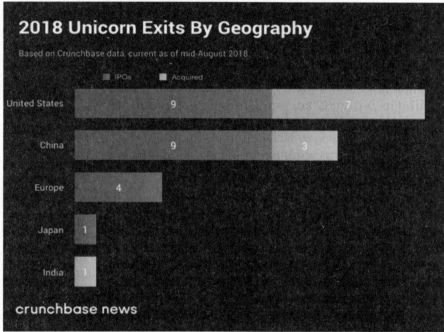

Source: Crunchbase

This Figure illustrates global unicorn* exits, as of mid-August 2018, and shows that China accounts for over a third of the world's unicorns. Together, the United States and China are home to over 80% of these unicorns.

(* unicorn is a term used by VC's to refer to a privately held start-up valued at over $1 billion.

INNOVATION

The **Global Innovation Index** (GII) 2018, co-published by WIPO, Cornell University, INSEAD and their Knowledge Partners is an index that ranks 126 countries based on how "innovative" they are. It considers key parameters giving rise to the creation and exploitation of technologies.

2018 sees China enter the world's top 20 most innovative economies, at number 17, the result of policy reforms, effected by China's leadership. Indeed, China is leading the way in technologies as diverse as, Artificial Intelligence, Internet, and New Energy, with Chinese companies such as Alibaba (on line trading), Baidu (internet), BGI (genome sequencing) and Huawei (telecommunication) now recognised internationally. For benchmarking purposes, Switzerland is 1st, UK 4th, United States 6th and Japan 13th, with other emerging economies, such as India and Brazil a long way behind at 57th and 64th respectively.

World Intellectual Property Organization's (WIPO) Director General made the following comments on China's rise up the rankings:

"China's rapid rise reflects a strategic direction set from the top leadership to developing world-class capacity in innovation and to moving the structural basis of the economy to more knowledge-intensive industries that rely on innovation to maintain competitive advantage."

A consequence of developing world class innovation is a necessity to strengthen Intellectual Property Rights from both a protection and enforcement perspective.

Returning to a more detailed analysis of the seven key parameters assessed by the GII, there are some very significant findings which should influence how a company answers the question posed in the introduction.

In **Knowledge and Technology Outputs** China ranked 5th overall. More significantly they ranked 1st for high-tech exports, 2nd for knowledge impact, and 4th for knowledge creation. When it came to Intellectual Property parameters, China was ranked 1st for patent and utility patent filings but only 18th for PCT filings (a route for internationalising patents). This indicates that many domestic filings may currently lack quality.

In **Business Sophistication** China ranked 9th overall. Again, more significantly, they ranked 1st for knowledge workers, 2nd for R&D financed by business, and 3rd for high-tech imports. Despite this, when it comes to innovation linkages, China only came 58th in the world, an indication that there is a massive opportunity for joint ventures and strategic alliances.

Innovation is no longer an option, it's a necessity.

ACCESS *to* INNOVATION

Practical results-focused innovation for your business

We're helping partners like Tata Motors, National Express, Gymshark, the NHS and Barclays innovate at speed. We can help you do the same. Join our Serendip 'Access to Innovation' programme at the UK's largest home for digital technology businesses to solve your company's big challenges. Find and deliver the Next Big Thing, drive operational efficiencies and delight your customers using our massive SME network and expert facilitation. We can help you have the right conversations with the right people, provide a flexible working space for your colleagues and introduce you to an incredible network of innovators.
Find out more at: www.innovationbham.com/accessinnovation

Imitation isn't always the sincerest form of flattery!

Intellectual property (IP) describes a multitude of rights, including patents, trademarks, designs, copyrights, trade secrets and domain names and for many businesses their IP constitutes a growing proportion of their business wealth.

How would your business cope if your IP was disputed?
Any business can be adversely affected by IP disputes. IP litigation can be disruptive, expensive and even ruinous. If rights are infringed, it is important for IP owners to seek resolution.

Protecting against IP disputes
Specialist IP insurance will not only provide cover for legal expenses incurred in defending or enforcing IP rights but also reassurance that your business is backed by a team of specialist underwriters, brokers, lawyers and approved experts.

Miller Insurance Services LLP is a leading specialist insurance broker and our IP experts can advise on all aspects of IP insurance.

For more information about protecting your IP contact:

Melanie Mode
T: +44 20 7031 2313
E: melanie.mode@miller-insurance.com

Graeme Lynch
T: +44 20 7031 2358
E: graeme.lynch@miller-insurance.com

miller-insurance.com

TaylorWessing

A full service international law firm, working with clients in the world's most dynamic industries. We take a single-minded approach to advising our clients, helping them succeed by thinking innovatively about their business issues.

"They provide us with a complete legal service, they are prompt and attentive in their working relationship with us and they make us feel a valued client."

Chambers & Partners 2018

 Technology, Media & Communications

 Life Sciences

 Energy

 Private Wealth

 1,100+ lawyers

 33 offices

 18 countries

Austria | Belgium | China | Czech Republic | France | Germany | Hong Kong | Hungary | Netherlands | Poland | Saudi Arabia | Singapore | Slovakia | South Korea | UAE | Ukraine | United Kingdom | United States | Vietnam |

taylorwessing.com

R&D Tax Credits

How we help Accountants help their companies or their clients.

- Recognising, scoping and describing qualifying R&D work to support claims.
- Auditing previous claims when there is still time to correct.
- Advising companies where HMRC have instigated informal or formal enquiries into claims.
- Situations where companies are using other R&D Consultancies and want to compare service/costs.
- Ensuring companies claim all they are entitled to claim.
- Making sure claims are secure as they can be enquired into by HMRC for up to six years, or longer.

We offer free CPD Workshops for accountancy firms on R&D Tax Credits

Helping more than 1020 companies gain in excess of £91m in benefit since September 2012

Tel: **01483 808301**
Email: **info@randdtax.co.uk**
www.RandDTax.co.uk

CREATION IP
turning ideas into assets

Creation IP is Scotland's fastest growing firm of patent and trademark mark attorneys.

We offer the full range of innovation and brand protection services, and advise on all aspects of intellectual property including patents, trademarks, designs, copyright and renewals.

Our skilled attorneys are commercially focused and provide a quality, high value service to help you develop your ideas to commercial solutions and get the right intellectual property for your business.

From idea conception to product retirement, Creation IP is with you every step of the journey.

mailbox@creationip.com
0141 5856472
www.creationip.com

aalbun is the leading global online IP Service Platform.

We connect our clients to our global IP network WorkZone, providing them with access to flexible searching and drafting resources thereby improving turnaround times, profit margins and quality.

In **Market Sophistication** China ranked 25th overall. Despite this, one can't fail to observe that when it comes to trade, competition and domestic market scale, the country still ranks 1st. For this reason, technology companies surely can't afford to ignore the exciting opportunities that this market presents them with and must consider how best to access it. Partnerships, joint ventures, and strategic alliances may well be the most effective way to achieve this access.

In the other parameters of **Creative Outputs**, **Human Capital and Research** and **Infrastructure** China still ranked in the top quartile, but its **Institutions** (political, regulatory and business, but not Research & Development, which falls under Human Capital and Research) ranked poorly (70th).

For those seeking a better understanding of the background to the drivers of change, and sector opportunities, they would do well to look to China's big policies such as:

- The Belt & Road Initiative;
- Made in China 2025; and
- The 13th Five-Year Plan for National Economic and Social Development (2016-2020)

the latter of which outlines the implementation of an innovation-driven development strategy to promote public entrepreneurship and innovation.

When it comes to considering the question "but how can this be done safely and effectively?" companies need to develop China specific strategies to manage their Intellectual Property Rights and form strategic alliances. The next section provides a brief overview of the key rights and some strategic points to consider.

INTELLECTUAL PROPERTY RIGHTS

China is party to most International conventions on Intellectual Property, but those looking to commercialise their Intellectual Property Rights in China should consider the following:

Copyright – China is a signatory to the Berne Convention, so copyright arises automatically without requiring registration. However, in China it is strongly recommended that key works are registered with the Copyright Protection Center of China (CPCC), and indeed, if you walk into the reception area of many Chinese company offices you will frequently see copyright certificates on prominent display!

Patents – In China, don't rely solely on an invention patent. Consider filing Utility models (a "mini" patent, requiring a lower level of inventiveness and providing a shorter term of protection) alongside invention patents. Also, consider using divisional applications to protect inventions in different ways.

Trademarks – China operates a "first to file" system, and thus it is essential to file key trademarks in China ahead of discussing/ showing products in China. Consider multiple applications to cover:
  i) The English name;
  ii) The Chinese "pinyin" name (phonetic equivalent); and/ or
  iii) The Chinese "translation" (where the mark has a clear meaning).

Since a trademark is a sign that allows a consumer to distinguish the goods or services of one undertaking from those of another, trademark owners should consider all aspects, not just words, as aspects, such as: stylisation, shape and colour may be more easily recognised by the Chinese consumer.

Trademark owners should also undertake clearance searches to determine that their chosen trademark is registerable and free to use before committing to it in China. Also, it is a sensible idea to check that the mark is "appropriate" for the Chinese market. For example, the number 4 is considered unlucky in China, as its phonetic translates as "death". In contrast, the number 8 is considered lucky, as its phonetic translates as "prosper".

Whilst China is party to the Madrid Protocol, and can be designated in an international trademark registration, it can be quicker, and more efficient, to file a national trademark in China due to differences in classification (trademarks are registered by class).

Trade Secrets – Businesses looking to commercialise their Intellectual Property Rights in China should ensure that Confidential Disclosure Agreements (CDAs) are used in dealings with 3rd Parties. Additionally, you should check that documents are marked appropriately as "Confidential".

In addition to the above, a company's China strategy should consider separate registrations in, for example, Hong Kong, since many goods pass through Hong Kong on their way to and from China, thus providing additional, or alternative, enforcement opportunities.

This leads us nicely to the issue of enforcement of rights, which historically has been a major problem for companies looking to exploit their technology/ intellectual property in China.

Enforcement

There are four formal routes of enforcement in China which are briefly discussed below:

Administrative Enforcement – This route is through various government agencies that have the jurisdiction to enforce IP rights, and can often provide a quick and low-cost solution. Enforcement is via the State Administration of Industry and Commerce (SAIC) and its local Administration of Industry and Commerce (AIC). Actions include:

- Raids, and the seizing and destruction of infringing items;
- Imposing injunctions; and
- Imposing fines for trademark and copyright (but not patent) infringement.

At present, this route of enforcement is most suited to trademark matters.

The Customs Route – This is primarily used to address counterfeiting, and provides a mechanism allowing an IP owner to record their IP rights with Customs (both imports and exports) on a national database. The owner submits their business details (company registration details and a translation), copies of the IP rights, a "white list" of authorised exporters, a fee and a power of attorney. For enforcement to be effective, the owner will additionally provide training to Customs officers at key ports and details of known or suspected infringers.

Civil Litigation – This is through China's various courts, and is becoming more common, possibly a result of the inception of specialist IP courts in key cities such as Beijing, Shanghai and Guangzho. Whilst it is incumbent on the litigating company to do most of the ground work, the court system is procedurally simple and relatively quick.

Criminal Prosecution – This is usually initiated directly through the Public Security Bureau (PSB), but a case may be transferred from an administrative agency (where damages exceed given thresholds) and is the most powerful of the enforcement routes, since the PSB has the power to detain suspects, interrogate them and make searches. However, the procedure is generally slow, and thus the former procedures are generally utilised.

The changes in enforcement, together with enforcers being awarded more realistic damages, see e.g. *Watchdata vs Hengbao* and *Huawei vs Samsung Electronics*, demonstrates that real change is resulting from the dictates of China's leadership.

Indeed, President Xi Jinping's key note address of 10 April 2018, at the Boao Forum for Asia, emphasised that the changes must benefit foreign companies when he stated:

"... We will strengthen protection of intellectual property rights (IPR). ... We encourage normal technological exchanges and cooperation between Chinese and foreign enterprises and protect the lawful IPR owned by foreign enterprises in China".

This statement goes a long way to explaining why, I believe, that the risks are continually reducing.

At the end of 2016, more patents were filed in China than in the United States, Europe, Japan and South Korea combined. In the first half of 2018, a total of 751,000 national patent applications were handled in China, and Chinese applicants submitted 23,000 international applications via the Patent Cooperation Treaty through the State Intellectual Property Office (SIPO), a sign of increasing exploitation beyond China.

Further, a consequence of the new specialist court is that patent enforcement has strengthened with 19,900 patents litigated in the first half of 2018 (up 23% on 2017).

TECHNOLOGY TRANSFER

On the assumption that the dragon is to be fed, when it comes to commercialisation, there is no one "best" way.

The three most established routes are:

- Transferor → Chinese entity;
- Transferor → Joint venture (JV) vehicle which includes the transferor, the Chinese JV partner and possible other parties e.g. local government and venture capital (VC) partner; and
- Transferor → Wholly foreign owned subsidiary (WFOS).

Technology Transfer to and from China, by way of a joint venture, has real tangible benefits for many although not all technology start-ups, and it is possible to actively manage risk.

Technology transfer to China is, however, subject to a regulatory framework, based on whether a technology falls into one of three categories:

- Prohibited;
- Restricted; or
- Encouraged.

If a technology is a restricted technology, an import licence must be obtained before the technology agreement is legally valid. Without this, royalty payments and technical fees can't be remitted.

For encouraged technologies policy benefits, including e.g. subsidies, tax incentives and government support, can lead to joint ventures involving a mix of commercial, government, and venture capital parties.

The risk that a technology, once transferred may be stolen, is, to some extent, mitigated by having a strong initial IP position and effective agreements addressing new IP. The management of new IP generated may prove challenging, and care needs to be taken to ensure it complies with the Chinese Technology Import and Export Regulations, of which Article 27 states *"improvements to the technology shall vest with the improving party"*. One approach is to ensure that Agreements specify that the parent company has at least a transferable non-exclusive right to any improvement / new technology in China, and an exclusive right outside of China.

Irrespective, choosing partners carefully, undertaking an effective due diligence process, and investing in the relationship, both before and after forming a joint venture, is essential.

CONCLUSION

I began this article with the question *"Is it safe to feed China's innovation dragon, and if so how do we go about it?"* I conclude with the observation that policy changes have resulted in positive reforms, such that companies should look to "feed the dragon", manage their Chinese IP rights and invest time and effort in identifying the right collaborative partners in China. Those that do this will ultimately prosper. To quote the Chinese proverb; 早(zǎo) 起(qǐ) 的(de) 鳥 (niǎo) 兒(er) 有(yǒu) 蟲(chóng) 吃(chī). "Those who are late to act, arrive, or get up tend to miss opportunities already seized by those who came earlier."

1.5

APPRECIATIVE INQUIRY

Charlie Wilson, Bosideon Consulting Ltd

INTRODUCTION

Appreciative Inquiry (AI) is a powerful way to generate positive change in organisations. It works by tapping in to a source of motivation which is seldom used in organisational change. In very broad terms, humans are motivated either by towards-goals or away-goals; they want to move towards 'good' things, like food, comfort or companionship, and away from 'bad' things, like cold or pain (see Figure 1.5.1). Most change models work by identifying problems and solving them; in doing so they tap into the away-motivation. This is effective but has its limitations. People can successfully move away from "bad" things in different directions, which can make it difficult to maintain cohesion. And the best outcome away-motivation can achieve is relief, ie. "The bad thing didn't happen".

AI taps into the other side of motivation by identifying what towards-goals can be shared by everyone. There will still be a need to solve problems. However, focusing on solutions (how are we going to get to where we want to) increases people's understanding of the issues and gets them more engaged in solving them.

Figure 1.5.1 – Towards and Away Motivation

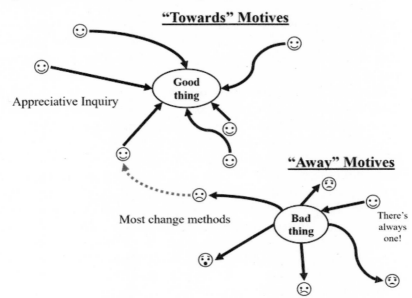

Diagram 1. Towards And Away Motivation.

It doesn't matter how long a particular problem has been troubling an organisation, virtually everything is open to change if approached in the right way. But sustained organisational change takes an enormous amount of effort. This can rarely be supplied by one person, or one group of people, alone within that organisation. Everyone needs to be engaged in aspiring to a better future and AI provides a way of getting that engagement.

HOW IT WORKS

Organisations work as much, if not more, by their social interactions as by any formal design or wiring-diagram[3]. AI helps to discover, understand and strengthen the social interactions that make the organisation work well and then harnesses them for positive change. By appreciating what is already good in an organisation, it provokes members to think about how it could be better.

---

3. If you want an intuitive example of this, consider the boss's PA. Do they appear in any organisational chart? Do they have any formal authority? Yet, how important is it to be on good terms with them?

AI is based on five principles (don't be put off by some of the names).

1. **The Simultaneity Principle**

    This states that even asking a question about a situation changes that situation; positive questions are more likely to produce positive changes.

2. **The Social Construction Principle**

    This states that we create our view and opinions of the world around us in continuous dialogue and cooperation with others.

3. **The Story-telling or Poetic Principle**

    Following on from the social construction principle, this states that people in organisations tell each other stories about what it is like to be part of that organisation. The collective memory of those stories and how they are interpreted creates the collective image of that organisation, the corporate culture in which people work. If the language used is positive, it creates a positive and energising culture. It is important to understand that these stories are not the events themselves but peoples' experiences of the events; different people have different experiences and so different stories. It is the bringing together of these different stories, melding them into one overall story about the organisation, which brings about the shared experience and creates a strong culture within that organisation.

4. **The Anticipation Principle**

    This is also known as the self-fulfilling prophecy. It states that, if people think something will happen then it is more likely that it will. Current behaviour is in part driven by anticipated results and, if there is anticipation of success, people behave more positively.

5. **The Positive Principle**

    This states that we pay attention to what we want more of. Furthermore, if people want something to happen then they will use whatever influence they have to help it happen.

IMPLEMENTATION

AI is a way of approaching organisational development rather than a rigid methodology. Its aim is to involve everyone in their organisation's high performance and so the way it is introduced to an organisation should reflect that. This means that it must engage everyone involved, including stakeholders. It may be that not everyone is equally engaged throughout but they must be aware of what is going on. The people who are deeply involved in the detail must come from all levels and departments in a way that deliberately cuts across any organisational diagrams. This creates a cohort of ambassadors who, when they talk to their peers, will create a sense of positive anticipation throughout the organisation. And they must be involved from the start. There is no point in some central power-group deciding on a change and then thinking that they will create an AI group that will go away and implement it.

As its name implies, AI works on the basis of asking questions. But before that, decisions need to be made about what topics to ask questions about. And before that a decision needs to be made about who selects the topics. There are a number of options available. They can be determined at the executive level. The advantage of this is that central management feel that they can retain some control and avoid difficult topics. That is also one of its weaknesses; if difficult topics are not addressed, perhaps the organisation cannot develop. The other weakness is that this cuts the process off from the knowledge, insight and involvement of staff, customers and other stakeholders. It is likely to be more powerful if the topics are developed by a cross-organisational team since diversity of input is more likely to come up with meaningful topics.

Potential topics might be proposed by the entire organisation and stakeholders. Whatever the decision, the earlier the whole organisation is involved in the discussion the better as people are more committed to ideas that they have helped develop. It is important that as few constraints as practicable are put on what topics are proposed and discussed. If a list of topics has been decided by a central team, it must remain open to challenge and development. Seemingly ridiculous ideas that come out can serve two purposes. They can allow people to "get things off their chest", which is energising. Also, a seemingly stupid idea, combined with something more sensible, can produce valuable insights.

If AI works properly, the topics chosen are likely to challenge the status quo. This can be disconcerting for those more comfortable with organisational diagrams and chains of command. This is not to mock or trivialise these concerns; change is often characterised as worrying for people lower down a hierarchy. It can be equally disturbing for middle and senior management, who might wonder if the organisation is going to change so that the skills and experience that got them to where they are will no longer be relevant. AI engages everyone in wanting to change.

Throughout this process there will be considerable dialogue and deliberation over particular words or phrases. These are not 'just semantics', they are an essential part of the process. As The Appreciative Inquiry Handbook puts it (page 41), in AI , "… a fundamental assumption is that 'words create worlds'; so the words chosen will have enormous impact". From the extensive discussion of possible topics, certain themes will emerge and those themes will lead to the choice of the "Affirmative Topics", affirmative because they encapsulate what it is that the organisation wants more of. They are an expression of the 'Positive Core', the energy that people bring to making their organisation better. Choosing the topics is summarised in Table 1.5.1.

Table 1.5.1 – Adapted from "The Appreciative Inquiry Handbook"

Topic Choice Rules of Thumb
No more than five topics are ultimately selected.
Topics are phrased in affirmative terms, ie. "Improved customer satisfaction" rather than "Reduced customer complaints".
Topics are driven by curiosity and spirit of discovery.
Topics are genuinely desired, people want to see them "grow."
Topics are consistent with the overall business direction and intentions of the organization.
Choosing topics involves all those that have an important stake in the future.

4-D CYCLE

Once the affirmative topics have been chosen they form the centre of the 4-D Cycle (See Figure 1.5.2) which identifies and drives how the organisation can change. The 4 Ds are:

- **Discovery:** A series of structured interviews in which people from across organisational boundaries share stories about their "peak experiences". In this way they construct a picture of the organisation when it was at its best.
- **Dream:** Based on the stories told in the discovery phase, people talk about and build a picture of what they see as a great future for both themselves and the organisation. Key stakeholders need to be involved in this stage.
- **Design:** In this phase, people propose the ways in which the organisation will work in terms of structures, processes and systems. How will people organise, communicate, collaborate and decide? What will they achieve? From this, and not before, they draft a vision statement about the ideal organisation. Including discussions of what is going to happen next helps to create and maintain momentum for positive change.
- **Destiny:** This is the delivery phase in which people implement the changes they have developed. Essential to this phase is an

understanding of the cyclical nature of AI: delivering the Dream and Design will open up new opportunities for Discoveries.

Figure 1.5.2 – The 4-D Cycle

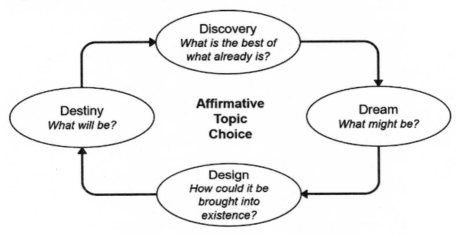

The cyclical nature of the AI approach emphasises the point that change doesn't end. Lewin's Unfreeze-Change-Refreeze model has been superseded by a need for continual change and development – don't refreeze. If an organisation learns to want more positive change, it will pay attention to it and so get more of it, creating an appreciative learning culture.

COSTS

- AI takes resources, particularly time. It will be ineffective if rushed.
- Participants need formally scheduled opportunities to discuss what is going on, to tell each other stories about what is going on and what is going to happen.
- Those involved in the detail of topic development and the 4-D Cycle need training in the techniques.
- Meetings will initially need expert facilitation.

BENEFITS

- AI's big advantage when it comes to organisational change is that it fosters higher employee engagement which leads to higher ownership of any changes. People choose to contribute and feel eager to cooperate.

- The process of deliberately putting together groups that cross organisational boundaries improves relationships within organisation and so communications. Important stuff gets passed around quickly.
- Improved communications promote greater trust within an organisation and a culture in which people feel safe to contribute their creativity and problem-solving skills.

SUMMARY

- AI works by engaging everyone's motivation towards organisational improvement.
- Organisations work primarily through their social interactions. AI harnesses these for positive change.
- AI is based on simultaneity, social construction, story-telling, anticipation and positivity.
- AI asks questions: care is needed as the questions set the tone.
- The more diverse the discussions, the more productive.
- The 4-D Cycle of Discovery, Dream, Design, Destiny generates a culture of appreciative inquiry and learning that generates continuous organisational development.

FURTHER READING

https://instituutvoorinterventiekunde.nl/appreciative-inquiry (translated by Google)

The Appreciative Inquiry Handbook: For Leaders of Change (2nd Edition, 2008). Cooperrider, Stavros & Whitney. Published by Crown Custom/Berrett-Koehler

The Power of Appreciative Inquiry: A Practical Guide to Positive Change (2nd Edition, 2010). Whitney & Trosten-Bloom. Published by Berrett-Koehler

PART TWO

MANAGING IP SECURELY

2.1

OPTIONS FOR BRAND PROTECTION AND DISPUTE RESOLUTION

Gregor Kleinknecht, Hunters

Brand rights enhance product awareness, quality perception, and customer loyalty and stimulate innovation. As the value and importance of brand rights have increased for businesses in a global economy, so are the brand protection challenges for brand owners and threats to brand integrity becoming ever more complex and global in scope; but brand owners have a wide range of effective tools at their disposal to deal successfully with those challenges, whether in a purely national or in an international cross-border context.

From attempts to use or register confusingly similar trade marks and trade dress for inferior copy products, trade mark infringement on the internet, through to conventional counterfeiting, product piracy and parallel imports, trade mark infringements by free-riders are no longer limited to luxury goods, electronics and prestige brands but extend to everything from medicines and cosmetics, through foodstuffs and beverages to car parts. It is therefore essential that brand owners are aware of their options for taking decisive action. Brexit adds further complexity and an element of uncertainty to the legal landscape.

EFFECTIVE BRAND MANAGEMENT STRATEGY

Effective trade mark protection and enforcement begin well before any trade mark infringement has taken place. A written corporate brand management strategy will help trade mark owners to identify and police trade mark infringements early and is an essential building block for effectively managing and reducing the business and financial risks which such infringements can pose. The strategy document should identify the brand owner's IP assets, the potential threats to those IP assets, define the means by which threats and actual infringements are identified and reported, set out guidelines in which cases action will be taken, what enforcement measures the trade mark owner will consider taking in what circumstances, and who within the organisation is responsible and has the authority to take the required steps. Another objective of a brand management strategy, effectively the reverse side of the same coin, should be to assist brand owners with avoiding infringement of third party rights. But the effectiveness of any brand management strategy is only as good as the awareness of it within the business – education of the business at all levels is therefore key.

CRIMINAL OR CIVIL PROTECTION?

The way in which enforcement action will be taken will depend on the circumstances of each individual case, or category of cases, the rights involved, the type and seriousness of the infringement, and the identity and location of the infringer. In some cases, brand owners will be able to rely on the assistance of the police, and of customs and border agencies in protecting their brands. This can have advantages for the brand owner in terms of costs, resource utilisation, and the scope and availability of investigative powers, and may in the right circumstances be the most effective way of dealing with infringement scenarios, such as a container load of counterfeit luxury goods arriving in or passing through a UK port, or a back-yard production facility for fake medicines having been identified.

However, the civil enforcement route is in practice by far the most frequently used for protecting and enforcing brand rights at a time when public resources are becoming ever more stretched. It provides brand owners with control over the brand protection and enforcement measures taken and the time required to achieve the appropriate outcome. Also, there are less clear cut cases of conflicting rights and contractual or licensing disputes where alternative dispute resolution techniques, such as mediation, provide a speedy and cost effective means of resolving such issues. The following is an overview of available civil enforcement procedures.

ADMINISTRATIVE PROCEEDINGS BEFORE TRADE MARK REGISTRY

In cases where the threat to a brand owner's rights originates from a subsequent application for registration or the registration of another trade mark, the first recourse available to rights holders is generally to file an opposition to such an application, or an application for a declaration of invalidity, or cancellation, of the conflicting mark in administrative proceedings before the competent trade mark registry, such as the UK IPO in the case of UK national trade marks, or OHIM in the case of European Community trade marks.

DOMAIN NAME DISPUTE RESOLUTION PROCEDURES

Likewise, where the infringement of a trade mark occurs through registration and use of a domain name by a third party based on or incorporating that trade mark, recourse to the domain name dispute resolution procedure of the body responsible for the administration of the relevant domain extension will often be the quickest and easiest way of enforcing a trade mark right. Not only do most of these procedures follow a common template, the Uniform Domain Name Dispute Resolution Policy (UDRP), they are also very cost effective and statistically tend to find in favour of brand owners in an overwhelming majority of cases. This can be particularly useful if the infringer is based in a location where effective legal measures could not otherwise be taken, or only after significant investment of time and money. If the panel dealing with the case orders the transfer of a domain name to the brand owner, no enforcement action is required at a local level in the country where the infringer is based; the relevant domain name registry will simply be directed to transfer the domain name to the brand owner.

ALTERNATIVE DISPUTE RESOLUTION

Mediation has become an integral part of the civil justice landscape over the last decade or so, and for good reason. The courts now expect all litigants to consider both before and during court proceedings whether mediation could be used to resolve the dispute. There may be adverse cost implications for parties who refuse unreasonably to take part in mediation. Mediation is a form of alternative dispute resolution, i.e alternative to court proceedings. It is a voluntary, confidential process of negotiation, facilitated by a mediator as neutral third party, and is non-binding to the point where a contractually binding settlement agreement is reached. It puts the parties back in control of the outcome of a dispute and enables interest based solutions. Where mediation results in an early settlement, it can lead to significant savings in legal cost, time and management resources. Mediation has a high success rate: although it can be difficult to persuade parties to attempt mediation in the first instance, once they do so, 65-80% of cases referred to mediation settle, depending on what set of statistics one believes.

Mediation is particularly appropriate where the parties wish to preserve and continue their business relationship, where direct negotiations have become dead-locked, in multi-party or cross-border disputes, or where court proceedings would require the disclosure of business sensitive and confidential information. By way of example, disputes concerning the licensing of IP rights, disputes over trade mark ownership, or trade mark opposition and invalidation cases based on relative grounds often lend themselves to mediation. Contrary to common perception, the more complex a dispute is, the more suitable it is for mediation, simply because the outcome of complex cases will be more uncertain and the potential costs and delay of pursuing proceedings more prohibitive than in straight-forward cases.

But mediation has evolved beyond the confines of civil litigation and the UK IPO now actively encourages the early settlement of IP disputes, for example, in trade mark cases through an extended cooling off period included in the opposition procedure, which allows parties more time to negotiate a settlement, or through a mediation service offered by the UK IPO's own team of accredited mediators at a reasonable fixed cost.

On the other hand, there are clearly cases where mediation may not be appropriate, for example, where trade mark opposition and invalidation proceedings are based on absolute grounds, or where the validity of a patent is concerned. Likewise, mediation may not be appropriate where summary judgment is available quickly and efficiently from the courts, where a party wishes to set a legal or commercial precedent, or seeks publicity for its enforcement action to deter other infringers, or where one of the parties requires an emergency injunction.

AVAILABILITY OF EMERGENCY INJUNCTIONS

In cases where the nature of the rights infringement requires urgent action, an application to the civil courts for an emergency (or 'interim') injunction or other measures, such as a search and seizure order, may be necessary and appropriate. Such injunctions can be obtained at a very early stage of court proceedings if the rights holder acts promptly, if he can show to the court that he has a strong case and that the balance of convenience requires an injunction to be granted to prevent the defendant until trial from continuing with the infringement. In appropriate circumstances, the English courts are quite prepared to grant such injunctions; they are powerful weapons but need to be deployed with caution and require a rights holder to be sure of his case – the potential downside of getting it wrong is a claim for substantial damages by the defendant. However, if an interim injunction is obtained, this will often lead to a quick resolution of the case by settlement without the need for further proceedings.

ENFORCEMENT ACTION IN THE CIVIL COURTS

The enforcement of IP rights in the civil courts remains a key weapon available to brand owners. As matters stand prior to Brexit, the English courts have jurisdiction not only to deal with infringements of UK trade marks but, subject to the rules on international jurisdiction, may also be competent to judge on the infringement of European Community trade marks, not only in the UK but also in other member states. Such a decision of the English courts will then be binding on the parties to the dispute and determine their trade mark rights throughout the European Union.

Trade mark infringement claims may broadly be based either on confusion between two marks, or on the reputation of an earlier mark. Basically, a trade mark infringement occurs where the essential function of a trade mark to distinguish a company's products from those of its competitors, and to guarantee their origin and quality, is undermined. This is clearly the case where somebody uses in the course of trade a sign which is identical with a registered trade mark in relation to goods or services which are identical with those for which the trade mark is registered.

Where a competitor uses a sign that is identical with a registered trade mark for goods or services that are similar to those covered by the trade mark, or where *vice versa* a competitor uses a mark that is similar to a registered trade mark for goods or services that are identical with those for which the trade mark is registered, the owner of the trade mark must do more to establish an infringement of his trade mark rights and must prove that there exists a likelihood of confusion between the two marks on the part of the relevant public. Adducing such evidence of confusion can be a complex and costly exercise.

Trade marks with an established reputation (also called 'well-known' or 'famous' marks) attract a higher level of protection. Where a third party uses a sign which is identical with or similar to a well-known mark without due cause, the trade mark owner may succeed in establishing trade mark infringement where use of that sign takes unfair advantage of, or is otherwise detrimental to, the distinctive character or the repute of the well-known mark. The owner of the well-known mark will not be required to prove likelihood of confusion in those circumstances, and the scope of protection of a well-known mark can be extended even to goods and services which are not similar to those for which it is registered.

The remedies which the court may award include injunctions restraining further infringement of the brand owner's rights; the delivery-up or the destruction of any goods already marked with the infringing sign, as well as of any advertising materials, etc., related to it; an inquiry as to damages in respect of past infringements or an account of the profits made by the defendant from the sale of the goods bearing the infringing sign; and an order to pay the costs of the proceedings, including the brand owner's legal costs.

THE IMPLICATIONS OF BREXIT

At the time of writing, the future trading relationship between the UK and the EU remains uncertain and a no-deal Brexit a distinct possibility. While industry continues near universally to champion close future ties with the EU that will result in as little disruption to trade as possible, and a transitional period, the UK government has published a series of technical papers in preparation for a possible no-deal Brexit. The implications of Brexit for both the civil litigation landscape (in particular, the jurisdiction of the English courts in cross-border cases and the recognition and enforcement of English judgments in the EU) and for IP rights are significant. While the UK's no-deal preparations seek to provide continuity in the recognition and enforcement of EU trade marks and design rights in the UK, and will continue to apply the rules on exhaustion of rights, at least for a transitional period, in the longer term the owners of European IP rights will need to apply for UK national registrations. Also, it is unclear whether the EU will reciprocate with similar transitional rules.

INTERNATIONAL STRATEGIES

How effectively a brand owner can enforce his rights internationally will depend on multiple practical and legal considerations, for example, on the place where the infringement takes place, on the level of control over the brand owner's local distribution network, on whether IP rights have been registered (if they concern trade marks, design rights, or other registerable rights) in the jurisdictions which represent either key markets for the business, or which the brand owner perceives to represent the most significant threats to his brand rights, and on the applicability of international conventions relating to the protection of IP rights in the relevant countries. Knowledge of the state of the law in other countries will be essential: for example, the French courts have taken a robust stance in enforcing brand owners' rights against E-bay in the case of online sales of counterfeit products, or against Google in relation to the use of Ad Words consisting of registered trade marks.

CONCLUSION

The key conclusion which any brand owner should draw from this article is the need to be aware of the different options for protecting and enforcing brand rights against different threats and infringements, both in a national and international cross-border context, and the associated benefits of obtaining expert legal advice on brand management and protection issues ranging from matters such as the creation of a comprehensive brand management strategy through to advice on the most appropriate enforcement action once a trade mark infringement has occurred.

2.2

TROLLS... REAL OR ARE THEY JUST IN FAIRY-TALES?

Melanie Mode, Miller Insurance Services LLP

Most of us will remember from our childhood the Norwegian fairy-tale collected by Peter Christen Asbjørnsen and Jørgen Moe, where an evil Troll sat under a bridge and tried to stop the three Billy Goats Gruff brothers from crossing, to get to the luscious meadow on the other side of the river. As in most fairytales, good conquered evil and the Billy Goats Gruff brothers dispensed with the Troll.

More recently, many may think of Trolls as those small, annoying, ugly plastic dolls with weird fluorescent hair, that hurt considerably when trodden on (but from which Hollywood has attempted to create a successful franchise, with a couple of films and a wide range of merchandise). Whilst mildly annoying these trolls are relatively harmless – apart from the irritating high pitch singing, which on occasions could damage someone's hearing!

As is usually the case the Troll film has a moral to its story which appears to be the power of inner happiness and friends. In this article, it is perhaps the moral of the story from the Three Billy Groats Gruff that bears the closest resemblance when looking at the subject of Patent Trolls, and that is "Do what it takes to overcome obstacles in your path".

Whilst the Billy Goats Gruff is a fairy-tale, there are many resemblances with the commercial world of patents. The Billy Goats Gruff represent the various types of patent holders, from the individual inventor up to a large multinational company or institution, and the Troll being a Patent Troll or a Non-Practicing Entity (NPE). The threats posed by Patent Trolls are very much real; they definitely do not belong in fairy-tales and could be considered the subject of a nightmare. Some have even gone as far as to say that Patent Trolls can discourage innovation and stifle competition.

BUT WHAT IS A PATENT TROLL?

The term Patent Troll appears to have been first used in the 1990's by Peter Detkin, a lawyer at Intel Corporation, who became infuriated with the many companies, who had never produced any computer chips, using patent infringement claims to sue the company for USD15 billion. Detkin actually used the term "Patent Extortionists" but when faced with legal action for libel he changed this to Patent Trolls. Patent Trolls can also be known as a "Patent Shark" or a "Patent Pirate", although the technical accepted term today is "Non-Practicing Entity" (NPE).

A Patent Troll uses patent infringement claims and the legal system to make a profit. They do this by obtaining a large portfolio of patents usually through the acquisition of companies that are failing, by purchasing patents from companies that have developed products or processes that they do not intend to use or by obtaining patents that individual inventors cannot then afford to develop. A Patent Troll, who has no intention of using the patents to develop a service or manufacture goods, will use these accumulated patents to threaten, from a patent infringement perspective, a company or institution who is successfully producing goods or services using similar technology or processes covered by a patent.

It is also possible that the Patent Troll will approach the company or institution and suggest that it enters into a licencing agreement to avoid legal action. The financial demands made by the Patent Troll are usually set at a level that the troll knows the company or institution can afford or just below the cost of litigation. However, the other threats posed by this legal action such as demands on management time are often so severe that companies or institutions will pay substantial amounts in legal costs or settlements to try to avoid or resolve the action.

BUT DO PATENT TROLLS REALLY EXIST?

In the UK it might be easy to assume that Patent Trolls may exist but are more of an inconvenience than a problem. However, a quick trawl through the internet and one can easily be convinced that Patent

Trolls are a very significant problem, particularly for software or tech companies operating in the US.

According to a Unified Patent Report in 2015, 64% of patent law suits were filed against tech companies and 16% against medical companies, with small to medium-sized firms being commonly targeted as the Patent Trolls know that the threat of expensive legal actions lead companies to make payment, even when there has clearly been no patent infringement. Back in 2013 President Obama, when addressing the US Patent and Trade Office, passed comment on the negative impact Patent Trolls can have on businesses and the economy.

Further evidence of the negative effect that Patent Trolls have on an economy can be seen in a number of publications and reports. According to Apple Insider, published on 28th August 2013, Apple had been subject to 171 lawsuits between 2009 and 2013. Furthermore, in 2011 a study by the Boston University of Law estimated that companies had spent more than USD 29 billion in legal fees and settlement costs, with the total cost to the US economy being an estimated USD 80 billion a year, when taking into account such things as lost innovation. In addition, in the Harvard Business Review published in November 2014, USD 211 million less was spent on research and development by firms that had to settle Patent Troll disputes. As well as significant financial implications to the individual companies targeted Patent Trolls have also been accused of limiting innovation and restricting growth of the economy.

Patent Trolls are more common in the US but this has been partly due to the relative ease with which the legal and patent systems can be exploited. For example in 2015, 45% of US patent cases were filed in the Eastern District of Texas due to the knowledge that the judge was considered a patent expert and favoured plaintiffs. Perhaps even more concerning is that in the same year Unified Patents identified that 66.9% of all patent cases filed in the US district courts emanated from NPE's, the majority of which were Patent Trolls. It is important to note though that some NPE's operate in a positive manner by assisting inventors make a profit from their ideas. In addition, reputable companies have also been in the practice of purchasing patent libraries, particularly in the tech industry. This can be evidenced when Google purchased Motorola Mobility in 2012, at a cost of USD 12.5 billion.

Another factor to consider is that the US legal system does not expect the losing party to pay the legal costs of both parties, unlike in the UK and Europe, and over the years this has resulted in many questionable law suits being filed.

SO, THIS IS JUST A U.S. PROBLEM?

Some would argue YES, whilst others would definitely say NO! There have been a number of proposed measures put forward to reform the US patent and legal systems in an attempt to reduce the activities of Patent Trolls; however it is believed this could cause the Patent Trolls to reach into new territories such as the UK and Europe.

Germany particularly has seen an increase in Patent Troll activities and this has been due mainly to the fact that proceedings for patent infringement and patent validity have to be dealt with separately. This process can make legal action more costly and time consuming and can often result in companies being prepared to settle Patent Troll claims to avoid such legal action.

Whilst Germany appears to be more attractive to Patent Trolls, the UK does have two weapons that can be used to try to restrict the activities of Patent Trolls. The first is the legal system itself, where the losing party must pay or contribute substantially to the costs of the winning party. The claimant may also have to provide security to ensure that the defendant's costs can be met at the end of the case, if there is concern that the claimant's financial resources may be limited. In addition, if a case is commenced but then discontinued that party will have to pay all costs.

Secondly, the UK Patent Courts are run very effectively with specialist judges renowned for their expertise who are able to review cases thoroughly and make informed decisions. Cases that are heard at the Patent Courts are handled very efficiently, taking on average 12-18 months from beginning to end. These two factors alone have acted as a disincentive to widespread Patent Troll activities in the UK as the outcome of legal action is too uncertain and could prove very costly for the trolls, if their actions were unsuccessful. Another minor factor is that the UK has relatively few software patents from which, as we have seen, most patent infringements claims in the US stem.

Whilst there are barriers in the UK to Patent Trolls it is still important to consider that often a threat of legal action is too terrifying for small to medium-sized firms and many will either choose to enter into costly licensing agreements with the Trolls or settle their demands. A Patent Troll may have no intention of commencing legal action in the UK but the threat is often all it takes to secure a financial gain.

Unfortunately, one other factor that could potentially serve to increase Patent Troll activity within Europe, is the Unitary Patent System (Single European Patent). Presently, there is still a significant level of uncertainty surrounding its introduction due to the Unified Patent Court (UPC) Agreement requiring ratification by some EU member states and, of course, the outcome of Brexit. If the UPC comes into being then Patent Trolls will be encouraged to commence patent infringement proceedings, as the threat to patent holders will be considerably higher because the decision made by the UPC will cover all member states – a patent could be invalidated across all states by that one decision. The risk for patent holders could be too high so many would settle before legal action is taken. In addition, the remit of the UPC could also include any companies that sell products in any member state and this could therefore have implications for US and Asian companies. Also, the lack of case law and multi-territorial judges could lead to a high level of uncertainty surrounding decisions made, which again could prove attractive to Patent Trolls. At present this is all theoretical, so nobody knows!

SO PATENT TROLLS ARE REAL BUT HOW CAN THEY BE DEFEATED?

Unlike in the fairy tale Patent Trolls cannot just be pushed off a bridge or made to disappear but there are tools that are available to patent holders to assist. As mentioned above, the UK legal and patent system does offer an element of protection for patent holders from Patent Trolls but what other protection is available?

When researching protection for businesses it becomes clear that it is relatively easy to find protection for the tangible assets, such as buildings and contents insurance to protect against fire and theft. Most businesses are also aware of the availability of protection against cyber-attacks but very few businesses are aware of the availability of insurance that can protect their intangible assets such as intellectual property.

Intellectual Property insurance can be a valuable tool against Patent Trolls as it offers comprehensive protection from the very high legal costs associated with litigation. It can provide the patent holder with a policy that can cover legal costs, damages, settlement and counterclaims. It allows the patent holder to make an informed decision when faced with a patent infringement claim from a Patent Troll. The threat posed by the Patent Troll can be seriously weakened by the existence of an IP policy as the patent holder, who feels that they are not infringing a patent, will have the ability to respond to the legal challenge.

As well as providing cover for the defence of a patent infringement claim an Intellectual Property insurance policy can also provide cover for the costs involved for a patent holder pursuing others, who they feel are infringing their intellectual property rights. In addition, cover may also be provided in areas as contractual indemnities and loss of profit, in the event that an infringement case results in an injunction preventing the patent holder using the patent.

As the moral of the Billy Goats Gruff fairy-tale states that one should "Do what it takes to overcome obstacles in your path", Intellectual Property Insurance is such a tool that a patent holder can use to overcome their own Patent Troll.

2.3

PROTECTING AGAINST IP DISPUTES

Melanie Mode, Miller Insurance Services LLP

Intellectual property (IP) describes a multitude of rights, including patents, trademarks, designs, copyrights, trade secrets and domain names. IP rights constitute a growing proportion of business wealth, especially due to the expansion of industries within the knowledge-based economy.

IP rights create a value of their own. They are often a catalyst for investment, and can be traded in the same ways as other business assets. However, regardless of the strength of IP rights, they are vulnerable to challenge by competitors and need to be protected.

Any business can be adversely affected by IP disputes. IP litigation can be disruptive, expensive and even ruinous. If rights are infringed, it is important that IP owners have the financial resources to protect their asset and their business. Here are four case studies showing how IP litigation insurance has been able to help and support businesses. The companies involved have taken steps to protect themselves, by purchasing insurance, against any potential challenges to the ownership, validity or title of their IP rights and ensure they have appropriate financial resources in order to pursue infringing third parties.

TRADEMARKS

'Company A', a web-based company offering online education, training and qualifications, wanted to protect its IP rights. Most notably, it wanted to safeguard the company logo, which was used to distinguish its services from other companies, and to protect its trademark against infringement. Company A appreciated that a trademark could not be an idea or a concept – it had to be something that could be "put on paper", or be capable of being "graphically represented".

Company A was concerned that the legal costs in pursuing an action against infringement of its trademark would have a significantly detrimental financial impact on the company. In addition, it was aware from past incidents that its customers could believe there was a connection between the company and a third party infringer, which would be damaging to its business.

The insurance solution
An insurance policy was sought to provide a substantial amount of cover for legal expenses incurred by the company if it had to pursue legal action in the UK and Europe in the event of an infringement, giving the company confidence that it would have the financial resources necessary to protect its business. In view of the nature of the intellectual property and Company A's competitive environment, it was established that the amount of cover required should be £500,000. In addition, to reduce costs the company was happy to pay a fixed amount of costs relating to any individual claim as an excess and also a proportion of any amounts claimed under the policy.

The outcome
Company A purchased the cover at a fixed cost which gave it the resources necessary to defend its brand. The protection ensured that, if any competitor copied the company's website and/or logo designs, Company A could take immediate legal action by instructing specialist lawyers to demand that the offending company "cease and desist" using its intellectual property. Any such action would also deter other companies from IP infringement.

LICENSEES

'Company B', a small but innovative audio products company, owned a large portfolio of intellectual property, including several design and utility patents, granted in the UK, EU and USA. Global licensing represented 10% of its income, and Company B granted licence agreements to manufacturers and suppliers of its products. One of the key issues faced, in relation to the company's licensee(s), was the potential for allegations of patent infringement from a third party and, in turn, the licensees were looking to Company B to provide them with protection from any resulting claims.

The insurance solution

Company B investigated the purchase of intellectual property insurance to safeguard their patents and reinforce their contractual position with the licensees. Crucially, the policy granted the same level of protection to the company's licensees, with licensee details recorded under the insurance policy. For example, if a "cease and desist" letter were received by a licensee, detailing Company B's intellectual property as an alleged infringement, the licensee could claim costs and/or damages from Company B, as owner of the intellectual property. Company B could then in turn make a claim under its own insurance policy to defend the allegations made against the licensee.

The outcome

Company B was able to reassure any potential licensees that, in the case of any allegations of infringement being made against them, Company B would be able to reimburse the licensees for any costs incurred in their defence. Therefore, both Company B and the licensees had peace of mind that insurance would be available to cover the substantial costs arising from allegations of patent infringement claims, court costs and damages. In addition, Company B purchased pursuit costs coverage, to enable it to take offensive action against any entity it believed to be infringing its patents.

CONTRACTUAL REQUIREMENT

Company C, a medium-sized spectacles manufacturer, was contracting with a large US manufacturer to supply its designs and license the use of its patented products. The US manufacturer as licensee required full indemnification, with a minimum financial limit of USD 10,000,000, for claims arising against it, due to the use of Company C's designs, patents and product. The licensee also stipulated contractually that insurance be purchased to protect the licensee's financial exposure to IP litigation.

The insurance solution

Insurers were able to provide coverage to meet Company C's contract obligations, including intellectual property litigation costs for any claims for alleged infringement directly against Company C. In addition, the insurance was extended to provide protection for legal costs incurred in connection with any contractual dispute, including non-payment of royalties, between the two parties.

The outcome

Company C was able to sign up to the commercially profitable agreement and earn considerable royalties from its licensee. The insurance fulfilled the contractual requirement and gave both parties reassurance that their legal costs and any resultant damages, up to the policy limit of USD 10,000,000, would be covered in the event of any third-party allegations of infringement.

Company C and the licensee also gained the benefit of advice from expert insurance brokers and insurers, who could instruct patent attorneys on their behalf. These industry experts were experienced in the intellectual property field, saving Company C the time and expense of locating and appointing appropriate experts itself.

GENERAL PROTECTION

Company D, an innovative company involved in the development of new building material products, was seeking to export to Europe, USA & Asia.

A prudent part of any company's export planning – whether involving products, services or know-how – is to ensure that potential intellectual property exposures have been properly assessed and the protection of IP rights considered. At this stage it is also essential to identify other parties' IP rights, thereby establishing the exporter's freedom to operate. A lack of due diligence in these areas can result in potentially expensive lawsuits, including injunctions from entering a marketplace, or the surrender of infringing goods and the payment of damages.

The insurance solution

Company D was presented with a range of coverage options. These had been tailored to meet its requirements and budget, and also its desire to retain a proportion of the risk.

Insurers were able to offer liability coverage options to protect Company D arising from its infringement of IP rights as a result of the sale and distribution of its products through other parties worldwide. Protection was also offered to Company D's sales and distribution partners in their export territories. In addition, a quote for optional cover was provided, to include pursuit costs incurred in enforcing the rights of Company D's own patents, design rights and trademarks. To reduce costs, Company D was happy to pay a fixed amount of any claim (GBP 50,000) and a proportion of any amounts claimed under the policy.

Company D's IP risk management procedures were key to obtaining viable and cost-effective insurance quotations.

The outcome
Insurance protection was successfully purchased, as outlined above. During the first annual period of insurance, the insurance contract was used, along with the professional advice of the insurance brokers, underwriters and their legal advisors to successfully rebuff spurious allegations of infringement.

CONCLUSION

With guidance and advice, companies can use insurance as a valuable tool to provide financial security and technical expertise to meet the needs of their business and for protection of their intellectual property. As companies focus on ways to minimise risks within their businesses and protect the value of company assets, the importance of using insurance as a cost effective measure to protect both tangible and intangible assets is becoming increasingly recognised.

2.4

R&D TAX CREDITS CLAIMS – AN OVERVIEW OF THE SME AND LARGE/RDEC SCHEMES

Dr Mark Graves and Julia May, May Figures Ltd

The UK R&D Tax Credit Scheme is an extremely valuable source of R&D funding to companies. This scheme is explained in more detail in another chapter and so for brevity here we will just summarise that it provides either a corporation tax reduction (for profitable companies) or a cash rebate / carry forward/back of tax losses (for loss making companies) based on allowable qualifying R&D expenditure. Allowable expenditure includes staff salary costs (wages, NIC and pensions but not dividends), consumables used in the course of R&D (materials consumed in prototyping / experimentation), software license costs and energy/ water costs. Costs of external companies / workers undertaking the R&D can also be allowed (at 65% of eligible costs) but there are detailed rules depending upon whether the company undertaking the R&D is considered a subcontractor or the provider of workers. This is a specific legislative distinction which can significantly affect the eligibility of such costs depending upon how the contractual arrangements between the claimant company and the external body undertaking the work.

Over the years the scheme has become more and more widely known with, according to the latest HMRC research (published September 2017), 26,255 companies claiming over £2.9 billion.

What is less widely known is that there are in fact two distinct R&D tax credit schemes:

i.   The SME scheme targeted at SME companies and subcontractors to LARGE companies (and some other bodies). An SME is defined as having less than 500 employees with either a turnover of less than 100 million Euros or a balance sheet of less than 86 million Euros.

ii. The RDEC scheme (prior to April 2015 the original version was known as the LARGE scheme, at which time the scheme went through a radical change to allow tax refunds previously not possible for large companies)

There are some detailed differences in the way the corporation tax calculation is performed between the two schemes. Broadly, the SME scheme generates a virtual tax deduction for 130% of qualifying expenditure, whereas the RDEC scheme generates above the line income of 11% of expenditure. Subcontractor costs are not eligible under RDEC claims but otherwise the schemes are broadly similar in terms of calculating the qualifying expenditure. Subsidised or subcontracted projects cannot be claimed under the SME scheme. On the other hand, the RDEC scheme is far less generous than the SME scheme: SME relief rate can be effectively 24% of eligible costs compared to 11% under RDEC, making the SME rate considerably more valuable, although the specific amount depends on the tax profile of the claimant company and nature of the qualifying R&D costs.

Many companies (and often their accountants) are only aware of the SME scheme, assuming that the RDEC scheme is only applicable to large companies not meeting the staff level / turnover / balance sheet limits and assume that RDEC tax relief is not relevant to them, somewhat understandably given its historic name of the LARGE scheme.

There are however two specific cases that SME companies should be aware of and claim at least some (if not all) of their R&D costs under the RDEC scheme; and by not fully understanding the RDEC scheme they can in some cases miss out on a possible sizable element of their claim value. *A correctly prepared R&D tax relief claim for an SME often contains tax relief under both the SME and the RDEC scheme, allocated on a cost/project basis*.

1. R&D Claims where an SME is receiving payments from a LARGE company

The first area where SME companies can make a claim under the RDEC company scheme is if they are undertaking subcontract research or development on behalf of a LARGE company or a person not within the charge to corporation tax.

Often SME companies *incorrectly* believe that because their work / costs have been part funded / subsidised by a LARGE client they cannot claim R&D tax credit relief believing this would be a case of "double funding". This is, however, not the case. The tax relief is structured so that LARGE companies who subcontract elements of work out to SME companies cannot claim the SME's costs as part of their claim with the tax relief falling to the SME instead.

One field in which we frequently see this happen and where it can be quite complicated is in the field of IT outsourced development, in which an SME undertakes software development for a LARGE client. We are also starting to see this happen in drug development, where a major pharmaceutical company outsources development to a specialist SME biotech company.

In such cases there can be multiple different scenarios with a huge impact on the value of the resulting R&D claim.

Another misnomer is that IP ownership dictates how the project / claim should be considered and we often hear companies claim that the project / claim is "theirs" as they have an IP ownership clause in the contract with the LARGE company paying for their work.

IP ownership was specifically removed from the legislation a few years ago and now determination of "whose project it is" requires an experienced advisor analysing the precise wording of the legal contract / commercial relationship and a detailed understanding of the nature of the technical work between the SME and LARGE companies to determine the correct taxation treatment. It is worrying that a number of advisors are emerging that are not sufficiently qualified or regulated to advise on this complex tax treatment; equally a number of accountants advise on the tax treatment without the necessary scientific or technical knowledge of the nature of the work being undertaken.

Consider the following possible scenarios:

Scenario 1: SME (A) is a subcontractor undertaking R&D for a LARGE company (B).

In this scenario the LARGE company B claims its costs under the RDEC scheme (payroll, externally provided workers, consumables etc) but not the costs invoiced by the SME subcontractor (A). The SME (A) claims for the same project, under the RDEC scheme for its costs of providing the R&D activity to its LARGE client (B).

Scenario 2: SME (A) is a Staffing Provider to the LARGE company (C).
Sometimes, the SME (A) will be providing named individuals to a LARGE client (C) to work on their project, sometimes in isolation, but often alongside the LARGE client's own internal team. Either way, in this scenario, it is likely that the SME is not acting as an R&D subcontractor but instead a source of workers to the LARGE company. Workers in this scenario are called "Externally Provided Workers" or EPWs. In this case the LARGE company can include the costs of the EPWs in its claim under the RDEC scheme and the SME is not entitled to make a claim for this project. Whether this is the correct treatment will depend entirely on the contractual relationship the companies are operating under.

Scenario 3: SME (A) claims under the SME scheme and ignores the LARGE company.
In this scenario the SME company claims all of its costs under the most generous SME scheme. The LARGE company may well claim for its internal costs under the RDEC scheme (or if there is no communication between the companies or their advisers may be also claiming for the SMEs costs as EPWs but let's set that aside). The key issue here is whether the "project" is truly that of the SME (perhaps with the LARGE company merely having the role of a first beta client) and not directly subsidising the project, or whether the "project" is essentially that of the LARGE company, with the SME working as a subcontractor for the LARGE company. Communication together with a detailed understanding of the nature of the technology, contractual payments, risk and warranty provisions can all affect the ultimate tax treatment.

Under these 3 scenarios, the LARGE company only benefits under scenario 2 (or 3 if their interpretation of the rules is such that they lodge an EPW claim) but scenarios 1 and 3 can make a x3 difference to the SME.

In such situations, advance planning by the SME can help to create the situation where the legal contract and commercial arrangements between it and the LARGE company can be structured in such a way as to make the arrangement more likely to fit in with scenario 3 rather than scenario 1, with little or no consequence to the LARGE company but a x3 increase in R&D claim value to the SME.

1. R&D Claims where an SME receives Grant funding (notifiable State Aid funding)

The other area where there is interaction between the SME and RDEC claims is where an SME has received grant funding (specifically grant funding that is considered as notifiable state aid). There are different rules governing the provision of grant funding that is not Notifiable State Aid and rules governing de minimus state aid funding not covered in this chapter.

Again, in such cases many companies miss out on an R&D claim, believing that since they have received grant funding, they cannot also make an R&D claim as this would be "double funding" or that they can only claim their unfunded element of the project costs - both are incorrect.

SME companies receiving notifiable state aid grant funding are explicitly permitted to claim eligible R&D costs on the project under the RDEC scheme (whilst being precluded from claiming under the SME scheme of course). They are only entitled to claim costs which are eligible under the RDEC tax credit legislation and so not all of the costs which are eligible for grant funding are necessarily permitted. For example, overhead recovery or patent related costs are often claimed under grants but would not fall into one of the eligible cost categories for R&D Tax Credit claims. Similarly, the remit of the grant may be wider than the R&D project for tax purposes (which will only cover the advance of science/technology not any related commercialisation, known application of science/technology or marketing). Often under high value grants there will be a Project Lead company who receives all the grant funding, and then distributes it to the various subcontractor partners in the grant project. This can lead to disparities in the tax relief between the various parties and up-front planning during the grant application can clarify or improve the tax relief for each of the collaborative parties.

Finally, the SME cannot include the cost of its subcontractors under the RDEC scheme. In just the same way as LARGE companies cannot claim subcontractor costs in their R&D claims, an SME cannot claim subcontractor costs as part of an RDEC claim for work funded by a grant. However, just as LARGE companies are eligible to claim EPW costs as part of their RDEC claims, so an SME can claim EPW costs forming part of a grant funded project. Again, advanced planning ensuring that R&D development work is outsourced such that the party undertaking the work is contractually an EPW and not a subcontractor can pull costs into the R&D claim that would otherwise be ineligible.

Undoubtedly the greatest misunderstanding that we see frequently is companies being incorrectly advised that they can claim under the RDEC scheme for the costs on the project which were funded by the grant and under the SME scheme for the internal self-funded contribution that the company made to the project. Whilst intuitively this seems logical and fair, unfortunately this is most definitely not the case in the case of notifiable non-de minimis state aid: if a project has received such grant funding then all of the eligible costs that the company has incurred on the project must be claimed at the reduced RDEC scheme rate.

However, this restriction is even more severe than appears at first and has caught many an unsuspecting company out. If a company has received any notified state aid on a project, then all future R&D claims in respect of that project must be claimed at the RDEC company scheme rate rather than the SME rate even after the grant funding has long ceased.

Real Life Case Study

Taking a real-life case study as an example shows just how serious this can be and highlights the need for forward planning and diligent experienced advisers.

Company A is an early stage medical device company undertaking advanced R&D in developing a new product which will revolutionise an area of clinical diagnosis. The company is a pure R&D company, still someway from having a product which they can commercially sell and all of their income to data has been from grant and investment funding.

For the last few years all of their project work has been covered at least in part by grants and they have always (rightly) made claims under the RDEC relief, not the SME relief.

For the year in question, the company had no grant income but a large amount of capital investment funding and made an R&D claim as normal, but this time claimed under the SME scheme, as all the work during the year was self-funded. The company expected to receive approximately £300k of tax credit refund cash in-flow.

HMRC enquired into the claim, requesting some further information about the nature of the qualifying R&D. The company responded sending some technical description, essentially describing their R&D in the qualifying period as an extension of their prior research previously accepted without question by HMRC and thus expected HMRC to quickly pay out on the claim.

Imagine then their surprise when they received documentation from HMRC informing them that they would only receive a claim about a third what they expected as the project was a continuation of a project previously partially funded by a grant and therefore only eligible under the RDEC not the SME scheme.

At that point we were appointed as advisors, with HMRC not

only refusing to pay out under the SME scheme but also with the company facing the threat of a penalty for an incorrect taxation submission.

Fortunately, one of our technical analysts had a PhD in a closely related area of technology in which this company was undertaking R&D. After a series of meetings with the scientists and engineers at the company and reviewing all of their historic grant applications and analysis of over 1,500 entries in the internal project time record keeping system we were able to describe the project not as a single overarching R&D project (continuing from the previous grant) but a collection of 9 individual R&D projects each with their own specific technological challenges.

We then determined the costs of each of these projects and resubmitted the claim with the necessary documentation to claim as an SME claim. While we were ultimately successful in this case, enabling our client to receive 95% of the full amount they had initially expected under an SME claim and only receiving a minor suspended penalty notice, the resulting delay in receiving the R&D claim pay-out of several months could have had catastrophic consequences for companies with less supportive investors.

As with many areas of company taxation, the takeaway from this example should be that a small amount of advance planning can pay significant dividends later on as well as greatly reducing the costs, time and stress of an HMRC enquiry.

THE WAY FORWARD

We advise companies to establish a comprehensive project / staff time recording system, which logs all R&D activity by staff and assigns the time spent on tasks in to grant and non-grant related categories.

We advise all companies to maintain a comprehensive log of all grant claims and submissions, so that the technical output of any prior grant can be compared and evaluated against the technical output of projects relating to a later R&D claim submission.

Furthermore, we suggest all companies planning on submitting a grant application should have the application reviewed by a regulated R&D Tax Credit Advisor before submission – so that the wording and costs being claimed can be analysed for their effects; on both current and future R&D claims. Specifically wording of the grant applications should use language which limits the technological/scientific aims of the project to that of the grant only and does not use language which could subsequently be misinterpreted more broadly to affect future R&D claims in a similar technology area as being a continuation of the grant.

When submitting an R&D technical report covering a project which has been grant funded in that reporting period great care should be taken in using language to describe the project as tightly as possible in order to avoid inadvertently prompting HMRC to adopt a broader interpretation of the technical aims of the project.

When submitting an R&D claim technical report for a company which has received grants in a previous reporting period great care should be taken in describing the technical project detail to ensure that it does not inappropriately appear to be a continuation of the previously grant funded project. Of course, if it is a continuation, then so it is, and the facts should always govern any reporting without inappropriate manipulation to favour the taxpayer.

If a company is also seeking SEIS/EIS financing, it is important that the technical description in the SEIS/EIS documentation submitted to HMRC ties in with the description provided in the R&D tax credit claims. Logically, appointing an advisor that is an expert in both tax regimes ensures continuity and no problems with either department of HMRC.

Finally, we advise selecting advisors who are Chartered Accountants/ Tax Advisors with years of specialist partner level R&D tax experience and a proven track record in HMRC inquiries (not just filing). They should also employ professionally qualified technical staff with detailed technical knowledge and experience in the subject matter of the claim. An experienced team providing both taxation and technical expertise can ensure the overlap of both are fully covered, minimising the risks associated with regards to client funded and grant funded projects. Discussing your claim in detail with the individual who will handle the claim will ensure you can assess first hand their experience, and not rely on salesmen's promises in this detailed area of tax legislation. Generally, in this arena, a respected firm has no need for salesmen as work comes to them from their proven experience and depth of trusted knowledge.

Note: For brevity, not all possible scenarios could be considered so this article cannot be relied upon as a substitute for professional guidance.

2.5

THE OPERATION OF THE UK PATENT BOX

Graham Samuel-Gibbon, Taylor Wessing LLP

INTRODUCTION AND BACKGROUND

Concept of a patent box

Tax incentives have, over time, often been used by governments and tax authorities to promote and encourage particular activities. In a number of jurisdictions, tax incentives have been used to incentivise innovation (and the R&D that is frequently integral to such innovation). R&D tax credits are one example of such incentivisation; another example is the concept of a "patent box", "IP box" or "innovation box"[4]. These generally operate by applying a reduced rate of tax to certain forms of profit arising in respect of the IP that is housed in the "box". A company's profits from other income or activities sit outside the "box" and remain subject to the relevant country's main corporate tax rate.

The UK government, keen to retain and improve the UK's competitiveness in certain industries including life sciences and the high-tech sector, introduced its own patent box regime that companies have been able to elect to enter since 1 April 2013. In summary, a company that is subject to UK corporation tax and that earns income

---

4. The generic term "patent box" will be used for the purposes of this chapter, being the name of the regime adopted in the UK, albeit that certain other forms of IP may benefit from the UK and other similar regimes.

from patents (and limited other forms of IP) is potentially able to benefit from a 10% effective rate of corporation tax (subject to certain deductions, described later in this chapter). Whilst the UK corporation tax rate has trended downwards since the introduction of the patent box (from 23% in 2013 to 19% in 2018, due to be reduced to 17% in 2020), the regime remains of potentially material benefit to companies deriving profits from qualifying IP.

Impact of global tax developments on operation of UK patent box

The benefits of the UK patent box were "phased-in" over several years with the full benefit of the 10% corporation tax rate on patent box profits applying from 1 April 2017. However, before the full benefits of the regime had come into effect, the global tax landscape had changed, requiring amendments to the UK patent box rules. Public perceptions and approaches to tax have changed materially over the last few years, with tax and tax avoidance generating headlines and becoming a hot topic at board and investor level. Governments have become increasingly concerned about multinational groups (in particular) being perceived as avoiding tax unacceptably/aggressively through utilising existing tax structures and regimes to "shift" profits into jurisdictions either with low (or no) corporation tax rates or availing themselves inappropriately of incentives including patent boxes.

As a result of such international developments, in particular the OECD's "Base Erosion and Profit Shifting" initiative and to align with its Action 5 Report on "Harmful Tax Practices"[5], patent box regimes in many territories (including the UK) have been amended, with an increased focus on the benefits of patent box regimes only being available to the extent the underlying research and development giving rise to the patented invention is undertaken in the patent box territory.

For an innovative UK company at a relatively early-stage of development these changes may not appear of significant relevance. However, they have resulted in a regime that can be extremely complex and where care should be taken, including seeking legal and tax advice at an early stage, to ensure that patent box benefits are available and maximised.

Encouraging UK companies to innovate?

In the case of an early-stage company or start-up (rather than an established multinational group) the comparative benefits of different patent box regimes in different territories are unlikely to be a key factor

---

5. http://www.oecd.org/ctp/countering-harmful-tax-practices-more-effectively-taking-into-account-transparency-and-substance-action-5-2015-final-report-9789264241190-en.htm

in structuring your company or group's operations. Within the UK, maximising the immediate cash benefit of R&D tax credits (discussed in the previous chapter), will usually be the primary focus from a tax perspective of a nascent company developing IP. This is because R&D tax credits aid cash flow at a stage of a company's development when it will often still be loss-making.

As the patent box effectively provides a reduced tax rate for taxable profits arising from sales of products incorporating a patented element, the benefits of the regime can potentially seem too distant. It may not seem a priority to focus or spend time (and money!) on ensuring that such benefits will ultimately be available and maximised. However, consideration of the availability of patent box at an early stage of an invention's development can provide a company with a materially lower effective tax rate once it becomes corporation tax paying, a significant benefit as well as an attractive feature in the context of a prospective buyer or exit.

UK CONDITIONS

Unsurprisingly, the UK patent box is subject to numerous conditions set out in lengthy, complex legislation and HM Revenue & Customs guidance. Whilst the rules are complex and legal advice should be sought by a company before seeking to avail itself of patent box benefits, a brief summary of the key requirements and how the benefits of the patent box are determined are set out below[6].

Qualifying IP
Whilst some non-UK patent boxes cover a broad range of intellectual property, to benefit from the UK patent box a company must either legally own, have an exclusive licence over, or be party to a cost sharing arrangement involving, qualifying IP. Qualifying IP for these purposes primarily means patents registered in the UK, EU (granted by the European Patent Office) or certain EEA states. Whilst not encapsulating a broad range of IP, the UK regime does also extend to certain other forms of IP, primarily relevant in the pharmaceutical and agricultural sectors, including supplementary protection certificates, UK and European Community plant variety rights and data/market exclusivity afforded by a European marketing authorisation. For conciseness, the below outline will assume that the relevant qualifying

---

6. Different rules can apply in certain circumstances to existing UK patent box companies where arrangements were entered into before 2017. However, this chapter will focus solely on the "new" regime that applies to all new arrangements from 1 July 2017.

IP developed and exploited is a patent. There have been concerns in some quarters that, following Brexit, qualifying IP could be limited to solely UK IP, but at the time of writing there does not appear to be any immediate plans by HMRC to amend the regime in this way.

Profits qualifying for the patent box rate

A particularly beneficial and appealing element of the UK patent box is the breadth of profits that can qualify. This includes profits from the worldwide sale of qualifying products, being products containing a patented component or products designed to be incorporated into a larger patented product. It is not just the income relating to the patented element itself that is caught (although it should be noted that anti-avoidance rules would prevent a patented element being artificially incorporated into a product with the sole purpose of seeking to obtain patent box benefits on sales of the product). Other income that benefits from the reduced rate includes licensing income (e.g. royalties) from exploiting a patent or damages arising from infringement proceedings.

For companies that have started making sales of products before the relevant patent has been granted, pre-grant profits can still benefit from the regime. A company can, in the accounting period in which the patent is granted, elect to obtain the benefit of the patent box on profits that have arisen during the period that the patent was pending (looking back up to six years).

Often a company will have incurred (potentially quite substantial) losses before a patent is granted or before the company is able to start commercialising an invention. Before becoming profitable, the company can stay outside the regime and accrue tax relief at the full corporation tax rate in respect of its losses incurred whilst developing the invention (an example would be R&D costs, although these may have already been surrendered for an R&D tax credit). There is therefore a decision to be made by the company as to when to elect into the patent box regime. This election can be made on or before the last day on which the company can amend its tax return for the relevant accounting period (generally, two years after the end of that period), so a decision can typically be made with the benefit of full knowledge of the company's financial performance for the relevant period.

Not all the qualifying profits outlined above will benefit from the 10% patent box rate. An adjustment is made to deduct a routine return (broadly reflecting the profit that the business might have made without access to the valuable IP; this is calculated as 10% of certain specified costs such as staff, premises, plant and machinery and other miscellaneous costs). There is also generally an adjustment to remove a "marketing asset return", intended to exclude from the regime the profit deemed attributable to marketing assets (as opposed to the valuable patent or patented invention itself).

Development of the IP

Readers of this chapter will typically be inventors and entrepreneurs that have developed valuable inventions and are looking to exploit them. Generally, companies in this situation should find they are able to benefit from the regime. However, it is worth noting that a patent box company must also meet the "development condition". Effectively this means that the patent box company (or an affiliated entity) must perform a significant amount of "qualifying development" in connection with the patented invention. This would involve creating or significantly contributing to the creation of the invention. The purpose of this is the policy of rewarding companies that have been properly involved in the innovation lying behind the patent or the application of the patented invention – merely acquiring and commercialising another person's invention will not suffice. However, the condition can also potentially be met in the case of acquired IP where the purchaser continues to develop an invention or a product or process that incorporates it.

There is an additional condition in circumstances where the necessary development outlined above is undertaken by an affiliated entity of the patent box company. In such circumstances, the patent box company needs to meet an additional "management condition", broadly meaning that it is active in the decision-making processes in relation to the development and exploitation of the relevant rights.

Development of the IP – modified nexus

Rules have been introduced by the UK government to ensure that the UK patent box regime complies with the OECD's recommendations in its Action 5 report mentioned above. The principal effect of these changes are that there are now rules that limit the income qualifying for the reduced 10% patent box rate on a basis known as the "modified nexus", the intention being to apply the benefits of a patent box regime only where there is sufficient "nexus" between the patent box company and the R&D undertaken to develop the invention.

In general terms this permits a calculated proportion of qualifying profits to benefit from the 10% patent box rate. The relevant proportion takes into account the aggregate of all R&D undertaken by the company (or group) or outsourced and including any costs involved in acquiring the relevant IP (where relevant). Broadly it is only expenditure on relevant R&D undertaken in-house or outsourced to unrelated parties as a proportion of this aggregate amount that will go towards the patent box company's "nexus fraction". That fraction can then be uplifted by up to 30%, effectively allowing for a proportion of IP acquisition costs and R&D subcontracted to connected companies to qualify.

Where there is a single patent box company that has developed its own patented invention over time, undertaking all R&D in-house or sub-contracted to third parties, the modified nexus would be unlikely to reduce the benefits of the regime significantly. However, in a group context, especially with any non-UK operations, care needs to be taken to ensure that R&D is undertaken in a manner that ensures the benefits of the patent box regime are not inadvertently eroded.

Development of the IP – tracking and tracing

In the context of a pharmaceutical company where a new drug is being developed, it may be relatively simple to track the R&D expenditure undertaken such that the appropriate patent box benefits can be identified (assuming suitable systems are put in place to track such expenditure). However, the position can be considerably more complicated where a company (for example a manufacturing company) develops and sells different products, each incorporating several different patented inventions, each with a different R&D background. In such circumstances, so far as possible, a separate nexus fraction needs to be determined for each product or product family, with relevant R&D expenditure tracked (for a period of potentially up to 20 years!). Obviously this level of granular tracking can be difficult to obtain retrospectively and it is important that companies intending to benefit from the UK patent box obtain advice and put in place adequate systems to track efficiently the data required to support their claim for patent box benefits. This can frequently seem like an arduous and overly-costly process to undertake for a relatively new company that is pre-revenue and on the brink of commercialisation. However, the benefits in the long-term of ensuring an appropriate structure and systems are in place can yield hugely valuable benefits, with a lower effective tax rate being achieved using a very legitimate and recognised tax incentive.

2.6

R&D TAX CREDITS – TOTALLY BRILLIANT – BUT NOT JUST A WALK IN THE PARK

Terry Toms, RandDTax

THE BIG PICTURE IN CONTRIBUTING TO INNOVATION

The total number of R&D Tax Credit claims made in the year to April 2016 was 43,040 – up 22% on the previous year. 36,820 were SME claims, up 23%. Total cost to HM Government of all R&D claims paid out or credited in the year was £3.7billion, up over 25% over the previous year. In rough terms, SMEs for Corporation Tax purpose are limited companies employing less than 500 staff.

These National Audit Office figures are never up-to-date for very good reasons, but at the recent HMRC R&D Tax Consultative Committee meeting we were informed that the number of claims made in the period October 2017 to March 2018 represented an impressive **increase of 44%** on the same period a year earlier. This places a massive strain on the gallant, hard-working civil servants in HMRC who process and police these and other innovation support schemes. I use the word "gallant" very deliberately, and with no tongue in cheek, not only because of the pressures they are under, but also because my experience is that in the SME claim world at least, HMRC Inspectors want to help and feel generally very positive about the real contribution R&D Tax Credits makes to the success of small businesses in the UK. In this chapter I will only talk about the SME R&D Tax Credit scheme for two main reasons. Firstly, around 98% of my firm's 1,020 clients are SMEs and, secondly, the financial benefit of the SME Scheme is so much better than that of the large company scheme. Exact savings depend on a company's actual Corporation Tax situation but, very roughly speaking, an SME will benefit from between 19% and 33% of qualifying R&D Costs, while for a large company the benefit is only around 8%.

£21.4 Billion was paid out since the start of R&D Tax Credits in 2000 – 2001 to April 2016 from a total of 240,000 claims. Again in very rough terms, this has probably supported in excess of £100 billion of research and development for both small and large businesses.

ANY TYPE OF LIMITED COMPANY CAN POTENTIALLY CLAIM R&D TAX CREDITS

We are often asked the question: What types of companies qualify for R&D Tax Credits? The short answer is that any type of company **could** qualify if they are investing money and/or time in attempting to enhance either knowledge or capability in an area of science or technology, or in other words, innovating in the way they operate their business – finding better ways to do things. The innovation could result in an attempt to develop a new or improved product, process, service, material or device. Figure 1 below illustrates some of the types of companies that RandDTax has successfully advised.

Figure 1 – Type of Company advised by RandDTax

Application software developers

Brewers   Manufacturers

Test and Calibration companies

Legal Firms   **Bailiffs**

Refurbishing of industrial components   Software tool developers

Manufacturers of machinery

Engineering companies

Ice Cream   Security Systems Software

Injection Moulding   IT infrastructure

Designer and manufacturer of industrial components

Winch makers   Motor Industry

Industrial process control systems

Financial Services Companies

This picture is by no means comprehensive, but it illustrates the variety. The two very obvious sectors cover all the massive variety of manufacturing, science and technology based businesses while the less obvious are professional services companies of all types including architects, consulting and environmental engineers and even bailiffs. Information technology based systems have the potential to totally transform the way companies and whole industries operate, while sometimes less obvious science and technology based activities can transform more mundane activities such as packaging or extending the quality shelf life of food products. In engineering all good companies innovate. I talked to one very small client this week who has just been chosen as the only authorised supplier in a niche engineering sector by the largest food manufacturer in the world because of the innovative technology they have developed over the last five years; and he talked about the importance of R&D Tax Credits in funding the work to achieve this status. I could fill endless articles with such case studies, and in this and very many examples they did not realise that they might qualify simply because they are very busy just doing what they do. One experienced owner of a Yorkshire based manufacturing company called me one day and said "I have been in business more than 30 years and this is the first time the government has done anything to help me".

After receiving a payment of just over £50,000 one company owner called me and said "my sales people would need to sell about £1m in value in order to deliver that bottom line result." R&D Tax Credits for SMEs is a totally tax free benefit and significant.

We often take on new clients who have either claimed on their own aided by their tax accountants or have used other advisers. We provide a free audit of previous claims where we are still in time to correct omissions. More often than not we will find blind spots, some very significant, where the company has not recognised work they do as qualifying R&D.

BUT NOT JUST A WALK IN THE PARK

In the UK our tax systems mostly operate on a self-assessment basis, much along the lines of HMRC giving taxpayers enough rope to hang themselves. We will often talk with companies and even their accountants, who will say things like "we/our client have/has claimed R&D Tax Credits successfully for the last six years or more years." Then HMRC decide to ask a few simple questions related to the latest claim or an older one and before you know it an official tax enquiry has been triggered. Where HMRC identify invalid overclaiming, they have almost unlimited power to investigate claims from current and previous years; and penalties can be incurred as well as overpayments repaid. While this process may seem unfair to some companies it is very difficult to see how HMRC could handle compliance in a better or more cost-effective manner. As taxpayers, none of us want to see companies gaining cash from our tax system that they are simply not entitled to claim.

ON THE OTHER HAND THERE CAN BE MANY REASONS THAT YOU ARE NOT GETTING ALL YOU DESERVE

What are some of these reasons?

- It may be that you do not accurately recognise that you are doing qualifying R&D.
- Even where you do recognise that you are doing R&D, you and your advisors may not fully appreciate all the areas in your business where technically qualifying R&D work begins and ends.
- You may be paying too high a share of the R&D Tax benefits gained in advisors' fees.
- You may be spending too much time and cost on the claims process.
- You may have made a claim or claims that HMRC have questioned, rejected or reduced, and you have lost confidence in the claims process.
- You may have set up sales or procurement processes which can make claiming full R&D Tax Credits either difficult or impossible.

THE SMALLER PICTURE

When we started RandDTax in 2012 our aim was to create a business model which delivered outstanding value through an innovative structure and business processes. In December 2017 we were successful in winning the Business Innovation Award, part of the National SME Awards. The judges said "Here is a business that is self-assured and unexpectedly using innovation to its great advantage". I did not entirely agree with the "self-assured" comment and thought that the "unexpectedly using innovation" statement probably referred to the mass of grey and disappearing hair on the heads of our founding team. Innovation is often seen as a young person's game! However, advancing age has been very advantageous for many unexpected reasons, not least of which is the outstanding pool of talent represented by our founders' offspring, in the breeding and training of a new generation of consultants. We are now a family business but not limited to one family. RandDTax now has 16 shareholders, all of whom are either consultants or in key operational roles. The combination of our very interesting and innovative client base plus good consultants has made RandDTax a very interesting business. Our belief is that this has enabled us to deliver exceptional value to clients in an R&D consultancy market which has become very crowded and variable in quality of service.

One of the largest and most respected UK owned R&D consultancies has recently been bought by an American company, and we have at least two Canadian owned competitors. Given the growth in the number of claims being made, we operate in a market which is seen as growing fast. Our growth as a company has been consistent, all claims have been successful and almost all of our clients were introduced to us by their accountants or other RandDTax clients. We do not employ telesales or sales specialists in a market where companies tell us that they receive more telesales and sales calls on R&D Tax Credits than any other service or product. It can be hard for companies to select consultancy partners in this space, and it is very tempting for both claiming companies and their advisers to cut corners in the claim process, thereby increasing compliance risks for those companies. We do not feel that printed disclaimers are any substitute for doing everything possible to ensure claims are valid when submitted. The result for RandDTax has been a very low level of questions from HMRC related to claims. In advising on well in excess of 4000 claims for 1020 clients over the last 6 years, questions have been asked by HMRC in less than 0.5% of cases.

Figure 2 – Funds generated for RandD Clients

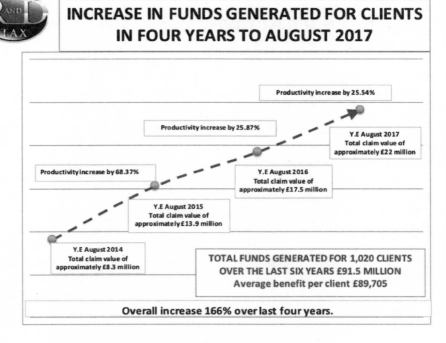

In Figure 2 above the graph shows how claim numbers and values claimed have grown for our clients across the UK. Because we at RandDTax focus mainly on SME companies our typical client is smaller than the average company claiming overall, according to official HMRC/National Audit office figures. Our 1020 clients have benefitted by an average of around £90,000 each and we have operated for six years. This means that we could have advised clients on at least 1 but up to 6 or more claims. The HMRC/National Audit Office figures suggest that annual claims are worth an average of around £50,000 although much smaller sums of money are often vital to the survival of young innovative technology companies; so our "war stories" include numerous situations where first meetings took place in humble front rooms or converted garages, and those young companies have since progressed to relative stardom – and the award of R&D Tax Credits has made a significant contribution to that success. If you are interested in looking into this aspect of R&D Tax Credits in greater detail, we have published a White Paper on our web site. This was the output of an MBA research project by one of our Principal Consultants/Shareholders. The title is *"Research and Development Tax Relief for UK SMEs – a good thing?"* and the author is Tim Walsh BSc, MBA, CTA. At the time the work on this was carried out Tim could find no existing study related to R&D Tax Relief which focussed exclusively on SMEs. Use this link: https://www.randdtax.co.uk/what-we-do/whitepaper

BACK TO THE BIG PICTURE

There are well in excess of 4.5million SME companies in the UK. In the year to April 2016, 36,820 of those companies claimed R&D Tax Credits for that year. I cannot believe that less than 1% of SMEs are developing the capabilities of science or technology to produce better products, enhanced services, more efficient processes, more powerful devices or much better materials. We see the brilliant results of UK R&D in every way, every day of our lives.

All companies want to gain real competitive advantage with new or enhanced products, services, processes, devices and materials. Advances in science and technology provide the ideal platform for this as we enter the Fourth Industrial Revolution (4IR), and that should be the main topic for our politicians to bang on about, when and if the dust ever settles one way or another on Brexit. Real industrial and economic strength comes from constantly striving for meaningful innovation – finding much better ways of doing stuff

– and I find that SME's in the UK are truly inspirational in applying, adapting and developing in areas of science and technology.

PART THREE
EXPLOITING IP
OPPORTUNITIES

3.1

NEW TRENDS IN THE IP INDUSTRY

Natalia Korek and Christian Bunke, Basck

IP INDUSTRY IMPACTED BY EMERGING TECHNOLOGIES

The IP industry has been around as long as we have had Intellectual Property Rights, with patents, trademarks, designs and many of the IP Firms around since before the Paris Convention (1883) and Madrid Agreement (1892). It has always been considered a risk averse industry as IP professionals have all been trained in finding the best ways to protect, defend and maximise the value of inventions, brands and designs. We have had innovation throughout the development of the industry and typically it has been incremental innovation and change in the way we operate. For those who have been around long enough, the shift to online searching tools and electronic case management systems meant a step change, which could even be called disruptive innovation, impacting all stakeholders of the IP value chain, namely: IP professionals, IP Firms, IP departments, IP service providers and also, of course, the Patent and Trademark offices, organisations and rights owners.

What makes this time so exciting and amazing to be part of, is that we are now at the next step change. We have disruptive innovation on our doorstep and we can either pretend it is not happening, and in doing so some will perish, or we embrace it and develop the industry further.

In our opinion, we are for the first time faced with being in a position where the IP industry is actually going to be impacted by new innovation and trends like Automation, Translation tools, Machine

Learning (ML), Artificial Intelligence (AI), and Distributed Ledgers (e.g. Blockchain). These changes will change the IP industry forever and change the way we work, file, produce, commercialise, enforce and transact in IPR.

Looking at the Gartner Hype Chart for Emerging Technologies (Figure 3.1.1), we see that many of the areas and technologies will also impact the Legal Tech and therefore IP Industry.

Figure 3.1.1 – Gartner Hype Chart for Emerging Technologies

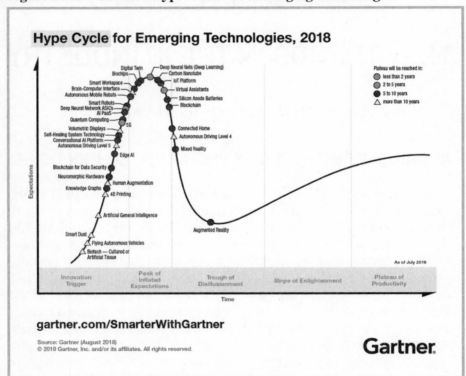

So instead of being part of protecting and licensing technology seen in the Hype curve, the technology will actually change the way IP professionals operate. The clear circle areas of Virtual Assistant, Deep Learning and many more, are all expected to be here in the next 2-5 years. This will mean the role of IP Professionals will move to a more value based consultant role and the very high end IP work. Days of billing per hour for process steps that can now be automated will become a thing of the past. Services that can will be automated within the next 2-3 years and arms length transactions that today are inefficient, based on old ways of working and geographical borders, will disappear completely or at least to some extent in the next 5-7 years.

LEGAL TECH DUE TO CATCH UP WITH FINTECH

It is often said that Legaltech lags about 15 years behind the software industry and about 5 years behind Fintech, and this means that we will now see very rapid change of the IP industry. It is said that people often overestimate the rate of change over the long term >5 years, but they underestimate the shorter term change. Looking at the journey that the Software and Fintech industries have gone through, the impact on the Legal (incl. IP) industry will be nothing but spectacular. It will not be just a disruptive step change in innovation, but more of a gradual improvement that will just transform the legal market. Even if IP professionals and lawyers are rarely early adopters of technology, we are seeing increased technology offerings and more importantly, investment into Legaltech:

- creating tools to improve data accuracy and data archivisation;
- pulling updates from the official registries to speed up the workflow;
- automatic translation of foreign documents provided by authorities;
- building mobile apps to communicate with clients;
- drafting support tools and quality checking solutions;
- case law review and guidance for decision making;
- using data to drive client acquisition and retention with new insights thanks to bundling external information with the internal data.

The impact on the IP Industry is still hard to fully predict, but with such a mature industry it will likely be incremental change until more disruptive change takes place in the medium to long term. We are seeing IP firms and IP departments that are already growing their own technology skill sets through using external consultants or setting up their own software units, which is something we have not seen since the emergence of IP Software providers during the 90s and 00s when things like standardised IT and Software solutions were often purchased in or outsourced fully.

This said, it is highly unlikely that it will be the traditional IP Firms who are the most innovative and disruptive as the industry evolves. We are already seeing new entrants into the IP Industry, both from technology solutions as well as new services providers. The difference this time is that the IP technology providers will most likely be building on existing platforms with their own algorithms and workflow solutions utilizing the most powerful Cloud solutions, Platform technologies, AI and ML in the market.

WIDER ADOPTION OF CLOUD-BASED STORAGE & SAAS SOLUTIONS

One of the major reservations that has been keeping the IP practitioners from migrating their data storage facilities is data security and, quite frankly, rightly so. However, having heard the story about the cyber-security breach into one of many embassies, safety of the non-cloud systems began to also be questioned. The hackers had been trying to compromise the system for months, and finally succeeded after having thrown an empty (or what appeared to be empty) USB-stick over the fence. One of the employees found it and out of sheer curiosity inserted into one of the computers. What followed does not require further explanation and shows there are always risks no matter how careful you are so again those risks have to be factored into any decisions.

The benefits brought by the use of cloud-based systems must be factored in when making a decision about the potential data transfer and security. Unlimited data storage and higher computing power allows the system to perform much more complicated operations, thus allowing for a faster adoption of new the machine learning and artificial intelligence algorithms as they appear. With the amount of data that each of the IP firms or IP departments is storing, the underlying potential in the use of AI and ML significantly mitigates the risks of migrating to cloud solutions. However, we see that many large Multinational clients will still at times prefer to take a more conservative approach with their IP assets to manage the risks of possible IP theft and litigation.

RESTRUCTURING WORKFLOWS AND THE POWER OF NETWORKS

While you can pick all of your materials, manufacture the parts, assemble the product and distribute it in the same country, the global manufacturing industry and producers learnt the trick early on. You cannot maximise the profit if you do not segment the work. Similarly, in IP firms / departments, the senior managers should ensure that the majority of their time is spent on building and optimising high value offerings and ways of delivering services. The segmentation of the work, however, does not by any means rely on seniority only. It is about letting people do what they do the best, especially if they are the only ones able to do that. This means that the hierarchical structure of IP and Law firms might see a break up as the power of networks and network effects (the collective power is greater than the individual parts) become more used to access the best IP experts no matter where they are located.

The lack of time, domain expertise and budget has forced certain IP teams to adapt their day to day project handling and add more consulting based setups with extra resources to better manage varying workflow. That is closely linked to companies looking to improve and maximise their profit margins by avoiding to have too many fixed costs and expensive staff, who may at times be poorly utilised. Flexible or on-tap resources prove useful for companies of all sizes, but we have seen the best results with:

- Small setups that needed to rapidly expand their practice after landing a big project;
- Big multinationals that struggle in some departments, and need to shift their resources to level the playing field across the organisation.

CHANGING MARKET DYNAMICS OF IP INDUSTRY

We are seeing new software offerings being successful by improving the old ways of working or doing better analytics of existing IP practices, through understanding of filing statistics and reciprocity of IP Firms and more: see the recent acquisition of IP data solutions from Practice Insight by CPA Global[7]. We have also seen the emergence of different types of new entrants in the IP industry. They often take things to a different level and are more technology focused start-ups with new algorithms, venture capital funded and even targeting a broader client base. One such example is Patsnap who entered the market by offering IP research tools and solutions to a wider customer base then purely IP professionals. They are now targeting to use IP knowledge to be a more integral part of the R&D process and are well funded by a recent $38M[8] D-round (taking their total funding to date to ca $100M).

There are also a lot of new IP Platforms being offered across the industry with most of the incumbent service providers all having versions of platforms to bundle their services on, improve the customer experience and move up the IP value chain. Here we can also see the greater focus on AI and ML to help improve the performance of the services offered. The industry is still working out what will be the real

---

7. source: https://www.businesswire.com/news/home/20180815005728/en/CPA-Global-Acquires-Leading-Data-Analytics-Solutions (access: 18 October 2018)

8. https://techcrunch.com/2018/06/14/patsnap-picks-up-38m/?guccounter=1

killer applications but good progress is already being done in better searching tools and IP professional support offerings. Two of the new IP Platforms focusing on doing things differently allowing for greater turnover and profitability are Pekama and Aalbun, both venture capital backed and founded in Cambridge, United Kingdom. Pekama is now working with building a community and managing all the IP work in one place. Great technology play that started from building one of the most advanced case management and docketing tools in the industry morphing into the Community it offers today. Aalbun, where Christian Bunke co-author of this article is a co-founder, is also a technology play that has come from the utilising of network effects to better access a broader talent pool of domain expertise and using software tools and their IP Platform of fixed price services to optimise across the full value chain.

IP INSURANCE WITHIN REACH

The premium that one has to pay for an IP insurance in the event of the intellectual property infringement used to be so sky-high that it was not even a subject worth discussing. Now, however, not only the insurance premiums have dropped to the manageable level (even £10k/year for SMEs), but also the way they work has changed. IP policies were intended to protect from third party claims against the covered party, but there are also insurances designed for those who would like to assert their own IP rights. Underwriting IP is still a very complex process but we consider the general accessibility of IP insurance as a huge step for both the insurance as well as the IP market. It finally levels the field for SMEs that usually struggle to find resources to litigate.

COMMODITISATION OF IP OFFERINGS AS FILINGS INCREASE

Just in the year 2016, the growth rates of the IP applications filed worldwide were as follows[9]:

- **Patents** – 8.3%
- **Industrial design** – 10.4%
- **Trade marks** – 16.4% (!)

The growth rate for industrial designs does not look impressive until one looks at the results from the previous years. There was even a minus growth rate (-10.4%) for industrial designs in 2014. It is surprising to see

---

9. WIPO Statistics Database, September 2017

that this relatively cost effective method of protecting products across many industries is not used at the same scale as are patents and trade marks. Sometimes misunderstood and definitely underappreciated, industrial design has come a long way and its importance is likely on the rise as product cycles shorten and differentiation in the markets becomes harder.

Trade marks on the other hand, have shown a steady growth for at least the last 6 years. With the growing popularity of commercial trade mark engines that allow TM owners to register their rights in selected countries by one click of a button, the trade mark rights have become a must-have, an essential, just like registering the company at the official trade registry.

The increased use of emerging technology trends in the IP industry will see all these IP rights becoming more and more commoditised. IP owners and IP professionals will have to change the way they have managed rights, look at the ongoing collision/merger of patents in the open source community, and delivered IP services. Hopefully this commoditisation will increase the accessibility of cost effective IP protection to more individuals, companies and communities as the importance of innovation and IP continues creating value for society.

Sources:

Gartner

https://www.businesswire.com/news/home/20180815005728/en/ CPA-Global-Acquires-Leading-Data-Analytics-Solutions (access: 18 October 2018)

WIPO Statistics Database, September 2017

3.2

PATENTS ARE NOT FOR PROTECTING INVENTIONS: THEY ARE FOR DOING BUSINESS

Dr Michael Murray, Murray International Partners

A few years ago one of my clients received a "cease and desist" letter from the General Counsel's office of an international pharmaceutical company. My client was developing an inhaled drug product and the pharma company held patents covering certain aspects of the design of my client's product. The threat was clear: stop development immediately or pay retroactive licence fees (going back 5 years) as well as future annual licence fees plus a royalty on sales once the product was launched.

The timing could not have been worse. My client had reported excellent clinical trial results and expected to launch the product within a year. It was their leading product and had swallowed up most of their investment funds. They were now dead in the water.

DOING BUSINESS WITH PATENTS

The pharma company was making use of the single greatest attribute of a patent; that is: the right to stop competitors from using your invention. Patents are business tools and this is a model example of how they can be used for commercial advantage.

It is true that patents protect your inventions, but the real power of patents lies in the legal right to block others from using your idea for commercial gain. With that in mind, consider the impact that has on the value of any business you build where patents support your commercial position. Without a legal blocking right, you face fierce open-market competition and your business is valued solely on its sales and inventory. If your product idea is good competition will be rife. However, with patents behind it, your business's net present value is many multiples of what it would otherwise be because for the duration of the granted patent term nobody can legally use your invention unless you let them.

Note the words: *where patents support your commercial position*. Understanding the full value of patents lies in this phrase. Patents should be crafted not only to protect your invention but also to create a strong commercial monopoly. More accurately still, patent *claims* should be drafted to protect your invention and to protect the business that you intend to operate. In the final analysis it is the patent claims that carry the legal force of patents. However, crafting a good commercial patent, truly aligned with your business model, is not easy. But as you are about to read, it is well worth spending the time and money to get it right. Fail to do this and it could cost you money, or worse, your whole business.

As patent applicant you are attempting to predict the immediate twenty-year future in your competitive field of technology and any associated business sectors. You are perhaps unsure which aspects of your invention are going to drive the innovation of new products or services. You may not even yet have a clear idea how the exploitation of your invention will actually translate into a profitable commercial opportunity. You do need to figure this out. A commercial strategy should determine the patent strategy rather than the other way around. In fact, it is critical to have a commercial strategy *before* considering a detailed patent strategy; or being more precise still, a detailed patent *claim* strategy.

Going back to my client; they desperately needed a way out of their predicament. They instructed their patent attorney to analyse the claims and produce a Patent Opinion. It was not good news. The pharma company's claims clearly covered my client's commercial development activities and would be infringed by the sale of their product. The claims were granted and therefore had legal force. From a purely legalistic point of view my client was in big trouble. Moreover, they could not afford to pay the punitive retroactive licence fees nor absorb the cost of future licence fees let alone royalty payments. It was over.

It is all about the claims

Patents sink or swim on the strength of their claims. Many patent applicants think first of the claims they can write around the technology. This is fine as far as it goes but it does not necessarily create a powerful business tool. Consider this: if you do not know what business you will be running with your patent behind it how can you possibly write a good set of commercially robust patent claims? If you have no clear business plan why go to the expense of applying for a patent at all?

Sadly for my client, the pharma company had a very clear business strategy. They were developing and selling a drug inhalation product. They had applied for and been granted broad patent claims. These protected their invention and could also be used to stop would-be competitors. They had already imposed this blocking right on several of theirs and my client's mutual competitors. If the competitor did not take a licence the pharma company effectively removed that competitor from their market (cease and desist applied). If the competitor took a licence the pharma company's loss of potential sales revenue was offset by income from their assertive licensing. This clever use of their patent created business benefits either way. Not surprisingly, they had been pursuing this assertive licensing strategy for many years.

However, they did not know it yet, but they had a problem. We had pursued a different form of claim analysis and had spotted something of crucial importance to my client.

THE COMMERCIAL STRATEGY – THE BUSINESS MODEL

If you are building or maintaining a vertically-integrated business with its own R&D group, manufacturing capability, global distribution channels and worldwide sales force, your patent estate will need to be sophisticated and highly articulated. You will have to strike balances all the time. Not everything that is patentable should be patented. Think of the value of keeping trade secrets, nurturing and protecting know-how, and future-proofing your corporation against the day when its key product patents expire. If you have valuable patent-protected products in the market your patents will come under fire from competitors. You will need a constantly evolving pool of patent claims in play in case an extant patent is challenged and some claims are revoked or in readiness for when you develop a next-generation product and need to extend your monopoly.

I can tell when I am dealing with a company that does not understand patents: their CEO or Finance Director will talk about the *cost* of their patent estate rather than its strategic value. If patents are just a cost to your business or you cannot articulate how they add to your enterprise, you probably do not need them. Either that or you do not appreciate what they could be doing for your business. When correctly deployed patents are an investment. The best-selling drugs in the pharmaceutical industry generate sales of more than $5 billion annually yet each single patent that protects this priceless monopoly could cost less than $2 million over its entire 20-year lifetime. Even for a less highly selling drug, the patent costs equate to about 1-2% of the annual sales realised on an annual basis. In isolation from a commercial plan patents will not add value or generate revenue; instead, they will drain company finances and will devour management time.

One company I joined many years ago had a "patent-everything-that-is-patentable" policy. The idea was to stimulate inventiveness. As a result, the company had twice the number of patents it needed for its business. I culled 50% of the entire company patent estate in a single year with a massive saving in costs. We were able to execute the company's core business perfectly well with 50% of the original estate.

Apart from the needless cost, a mindless patenting policy can lead to potentially valuable intellectual capital being disclosed prematurely. Patent applications are automatically published. In most jurisdictions patent applications are made available to the public 18 months after the initial filing date (or sooner in some circumstances). Once in the public domain that secret is out, never to be retrieved. Think of the often-quoted example of the *Coca Cola®* recipe. Had this been patented the world's most famous recipe would have been legally available for commercial use by third parties more than a century ago. As it is, the recipe, a trade secret, is reputed to be known by fewer than a handful of individuals and the company's lead product maintains a dominant position in the market to this day. The profits are not bad either.

THE PHARMA COMPANY'S PROBLEM

So back to my troubled client: How could a well-resourced pharma company with broad patent claims and a highly remunerative assertive licensing strategy possibly have a problem? Their own product was selling well. They had numerous licensees who had been ensnared by the very breadth of their granted patent claims. Consequently, they were receiving revenue in the form of their own product sales, third party licence fees and third party royalties.

Paradoxically, the breadth of their claims was the problem. The scope of granted patent claims should be commensurate with the extent of the disclosure by the patentee. We could see that the pharma company had been granted claims that could not be supported by the technical disclosure made in their patent specification. In short: many of their claims were invalid; crucially, the claims that purportedly affected my client.

Of course, the pharma company's commercial strategy relied heavily on these broad, yet invalid, claims but assertive licensing had not driven their initial patent claim strategy. Rather, they had originally written claims aimed at protecting their own invention; the breadth of the claims was principally to create a buffer zone of intellectual property rights around it. The assertive licensing campaign came much later. It was opportunist. But because it was not the originally intended use of the patent, their claims were not supported by an adequate level of disclosure and data. They were not fit for this particular commercial purpose.

The business solution
The pharma company's claims were susceptible to challenge. They could not risk a public defence of their patent because there was the risk that they might lose not only the unjustifiably broad claims but also the core claims which protected their product. They simply did not want us to challenge their patent.

We were able to negotiate a licence in perpetuity subject to my client not launching a patent challenge. No fees were paid.

The pharma company did not expose their patent to an invalidity claim. My client dodged the punitive historical and future licence fees, and future royalty payments. Both the pharma company's and my client's mutual competitors continued to pay the pharma company the licence fees (since the patent and its claims remained in force) providing a commercial advantage both to my client – their competitors had a significant extra cost base due to the licence fees they were paying, and to the pharma company – their product IP was intact and they still received third party income.

SUMMING UP

Inventions are the engines of innovation. It is innovation which turns the business potential, embedded somewhere in the invention, into a business opportunity. Patents can be limited in scope if their claims are predicated only on the invention itself or are not aligned with the business model through which they will be monetised. By taking account of the ensuing innovations and the manner in which they are likely to be commercially exploited patent claims can be transformed into truly potent and valuable business tools.

3.3

THE IMPACT OF GENERAL DATA PROTECTION REGULATION GDPR ON IP WORK

Margit Hoehne, patentGate GmbH

The General Data Protection Regulation GDPR has entered into force on May 25th, 2018. All companies are concerned when they collect, store and use personal data of EU citizens. This has an impact on IP work, because personal data of inventors, licensors or licensees within or outside the company is processed and must be made available to organizations domestically and abroad.

This chapter describes basic information about the GDPR and then shows how that applies in an application to record, manage and revise a company's inventions that is a module of the patent monitoring application patentGate.

WHAT IS THE GDPR?

The EU Regulation 2016/679 from April 27th, 2016 on the protection of natural persons with regard to the processing of personal data and on the free movement of such data, and repealing Directive 95/46/EC (General Data Protection Regulation) was enacted on May 25th, 2018. It is a binding legislative act and is validated EU-wide without the ratification of the EU member states.

The aim of the GDPR is to protect personal data of EU citizens and allow for more transparency regarding which data is stored, if it is given to others, as well as possibilities to correct and delete data.

Who is concerned?

All companies who collect, store or use personal data of European Union citizens have to comply with the GDPR. It is unimportant if the company concerned has a location or a representative within the EU.

IP departments often communicate with foreign patent attorneys, offices and cooperation partners worldwide and it is necessary for them to obtain and use personal data.

What is personal data?

Personal data is all data concering an individual, like name, communication details (address, phone, e-mail...), date of birth, bank details, but also twitter handles, social media user names or IP addresses.

When is it allowed to process personal data?

According to Article 6 of the GDPR processing is lawful if at least one of six rules apply:

- If using the personal data is necessary to fulfill a contract with the person concerned or the preparation of such a contract, then the processing is allowed. The same applies, for instance, if the personal data is processed to comply with legal obligations, to carry out a task in the public interest or to protect the vital interests of any natural person.
- In all cases not defined in Article 6 1(b) to 1(f) explicit consent of the person concerned is necessary and must be documented.
- If the data subject has given consent to the processing of their personal data for specific purposes then the personal data may be used for those purposes only.

Where, how and why is data processed?

The GDPR requires to make sure to protect the rights of the persons concerned. They have to be informed about the collected data and be given opportunity to make corrections.

A person can withdraw the explicit consent given under Article 6 (a) at any time and without explanation. They have a "right to forget" which guarantees that all data must be deleted without traces. The technical implementation of that is a challenge, because this also includes backup copies or document management systems with revision control functions.

All data stored should be protected from access of unauthorized persons. This can be done with encryption, password protection and access restrictions.

Which actions are necessary?

The GDPR demands accountability for all processes involving personal data.

The first step is to analyse which processes work with personal data and which measures are to be taken to adapt those processes, when the need arises. If consent is necessary because the processing of the data is not or not yet covered in the contractual relationship, the data subject must be informed and asked about the process. This is an opt-in-porcedure; an explicit, voluntary action to consent that data is saved and processed.

Accountability requirements (detified in Figure 3.3.1) also include documenting the data protection measures in all relevant processes and risk assessment to show that you work with due diligence.

- If the data is stored in the EU, GDPR requirements must be met. If data of EU citizens is stored outside of the EU, those rules apply as well. As long as the UK is an EU member state, the GDPR is valid there. After Brexit the UK will probaby still comply to the GDPR, and therefor will be treated like an EU member state. To store data in third party states the service provider should prove that the protection level for personal data is similar to the standards within the EU. This can be proven by a certificate issued by the European Commission.
- GDPR increases the responsibility of organizations which store and work with personal data; the person concerned should be informed better about what will happen with their data. These processes are to be described in a company's privacy policy.
- Every person may inquire about the personal data stored about them. In some cases they can withdraw their consent about data storage and processing. If the person deems corrections necessary, they have to be implemented. If the contractual relationship is ended and no other laws require the storage of data, a user may request the deletion of all their data.
- Employees must be educated on the impact of GDPR so that they can act accordingly. This training should raise awareness for all employees.
- Personal data must always be protected. Access control includes password protection for computers and databases as well as access restrictions to offices, which guarantees no personal data

is accessible for guests or employees that do not need to access this data for their intended work.

- Only persons who require access to personal data for their tasks are allowed to view and modify the personal data.
- Steps have to be taken to prevent breaches in data protection. A reporting system must be installed which informs authorities and affected users within 72 hours, if a loss of 1data occurs.

In an audit all the measures taken should be transparent.

Figure 3.3.1 – GDPR Accountabilty

Data protection principles
The GDPR defines in Article 25 that information systems should afford two concepts: privacy by design and privacy by default.

- Privacy by default means that default options should afford the maximum privacy and protect users from unwanted offers or newsletters.
- When an application is designed with "Privacy by design", it means that the data protection measures are already implemented in the design process and the users will have to opt in for additional options, for instance to subscribe to an email newsletter.

INVENTION MANAGEMENT IN PATENTGATE

PatentGate is a patent monitoring application that helps you to monitor current intellectual property rights. Technology trends and inventions of competitors are selected based on search profiles. The patent documents can be distributed and evaluated. Company specific search fields, patent families, citations, and legal status information complete the database.

The main content of the monitoring database is publicly available data that has been published by patent organizations. Inventors' private address data is not stored in the database, even if it is available in the data published by the patent authorities.

The monitoring workflow, where engineers and R&D employees comment on the patent documents, does contain some personal data of the employee – for instance the email address to receive notifications. If a comment is made the author and date of the comment are stored in the database, because that is necessary for the monitoring procedure.

Another aspect of patent information focusses on a company's own inventions. It shows appreciation for the inventors and informs them about the life cycle of patent applications based on their inventions. In that case more personal data is required.

Invention questionnaire

A web-based questionnaire collects information about the invention, the date the invention was made, which preliminary knowledge influenced the invention (state of the art IP rights, other publications, brochures, trade fair catalogues) and information about the inventors.

The layout and the questions asked are adapted to the company using the questionnaire. It consists of informational texts, boxes to insert text, drop down boxes, checkboxes or radio buttons to define different input options, so that complex topics can be adapted.

The workflow allows the questionnaire to be saved as a draft, and to be sent to the IP department when all necessary questions have been answered. After sending the questionnaire the date of the invention and an internal file number will be assigned to the invention. Additional documents (drawings, texts) can be uploaded.

The IP department can review the invention and send it back to the inventors, if there is information missing. A timeline can be assigned in which the missing data has to be completed.

If all data is complete, the invention can be sent to a patent attorney or patent searcher who starts a novelty search and informs the IP department about the search result. Those results are made available in the database or as a PDF report connected to the invention.

Based on the search result the IP department and management can decide if the invention will be filed with the company as the patent assignee or if the inventor can do so himself. The decision is linked to the invention. Letters or emails are prepared to inform the inventor about this decision. Those are linked to the invention as well so that all information regarding an invention is available at one single source.

If the company has various international offices with different legislations for inventor renumeration and filing systems, the questionnaire's and letter's content can be adapted depending on the country of the inventor's employment.

Other modules also work with the personal data of inventors. To ensure the privacy of inventors no address data is published in patentGate's public patent databases; only the name and country of residence.

When information about filed patent applications that have not yet been published is made available in a company's database, access will be restricted only to the users involved in this invention. The IP department can share all or selected unpublished files for different users.

Access to those files can be restricted before the date of the official publication, so that only the inventor(s) and IP professionals can view the current documents attached to the invention such as the claims that have been filed.

When the patent application is published by the IP office there will be links between the internal file and the patent document and public information will be made available without restriction.

Challenges of the GDPR

Patent authorities require the name and private address of all inventors for a patent application. That data will also be transferred to patent attorneys that represent the company worldwide, if more than a national patent application is planned. That's why those lawyers must make sure that the personal data of the inventors is protected as it would be within the EU.

Inventors are not necessarily employees, but they can also work for cooperating university departments or companies, or are short term employees like students or postgraduates. As it takes 18 months after the filing date for a patent application to be published and even longer to grant the patent, some employees will not be with the company anymore at a time when further steps in the patent granting procedure are taken.

The personal data of those former employees is necessary for the performance of a contract and compliance with a legal obligation under Article 6 1(b or c) to calculate inventor remuneration or communicate with the patent authorities.

To comply with GDPR, patentGate gives the inventor the option to store his or her private address data and communication details in the application, granting the IP department access when that is necessary. Other inventors do not have access to the address data stored, so that the inventor's privacy is guaranteed.

Depending on the contract between inventor and patent applicant there can be contract clauses that apply in case of a changed private address. Then the inventor must inform his (former) employer or consent to a request to the population register to obtain the new address data. This consent should be implemented in new contracts. If an inventor has already left the company, an additional contract clause could be added with the next communication between both parties.

CONCLUSION

GDPR causes companies to think about their handling of personal data. In many cases data is already stored economically, but it is also a chance to think about the protection of personal data and to check if some data is necessarily stored and processed or if it can be waived.

3.4

PATENT LANDSCAPE STUDY: PHARMACEUTICAL AND ENGINEERING EXAMPLES

Steven Johnson and Vedran Biondic, J&B Partners Ltd. – Patent and Scientific Research

We have seen before how information can be the key to a successful business and innovation strategy. The part that patent information plays can be essential, whether it is through the valuable mine of technical information included in the specification, or the insight into the activities of other companies and individuals in the technology field of interest.

In this chapter we will look at two landscape studies, one focusing on technical aspects and another focusing more on the corporate landscape. We will explain the different stages and strategies that can shape the search and analysis, and give an idea of where the value lies in the output.

We have chosen two topics, one in the chemical field, relating to a well-known drug, pregabalin, and another in the mechanical field, fully electric vehicles. We have chosen these topics as they are good representatives for the types of search we are showcasing.

LANDSCAPE STUDY I – PREGABALIN

Objective
The first search will focus on the drug pregabalin, also known by its trade name Lyrica™. The drug is known for treating anxiety disorders,

epilepsy, and neuralgia. We have chosen the subject matter for this first study for its suitability to provide a simple example of a technical based landscape, but it also represents a specific scenario where a landscape study can be a very useful tool. The original patent covering pregabalin is due to expire in 2018, at which point new opportunities may arise for exploitation of the technology around the compound. This study looks closely at the technical details of the patents covering all aspects of pregabalin.

The objective can therefore be stated as to understand the technical patent landscape relating to the compound. The field will be split into six aspects: synthesis/preparation; forms – crystal structures, conjugates and prodrugs; formulations – mixtures with excipients, tablets, etc.; combinations – with other active agents; indications – particular uses and treatments; and devices – such as for delivery or specialist containers.

Search Characterisation and Strategy

For a well-known drug the primary search strategy will be keyword based. All trade names and synonyms for the compound are collected, as well as strategies for covering the systematic names. In this case the main terms were pregabalin and lyrica, but over 50 other terms were found from different countries and for different formulations of the drug. Class based analysis does not lend itself well to this compound as it is relatively simple. For example, covering classes relating to amino acids would provide a huge amount of noise and would not be cost effective. Other potential strategies could include structure searching and even additional citation analysis, to further add to the dataset.

The choice of database is also important; access to the most up to date records and with the ability to perform all the particular types of searches is essential. Ideally a number of sources would be used to collect the data, however in this case the database used was PatBase^{TM}.

To give a broad picture the search was not limited by country or timescale, although all records relating to pregabalin should by definition, come from the past 25 years.

Inspection, Data Collection and Cleaning

In order to get the most out of a technical landscape search it is important that the dataset is as detailed as possible. Once search strategies are in place, the records need to be categorised; ideally this would entail a manual inspection of all records in all patent families. The dataset also needs to be as complete as possible for the field, for a meaningful study the dataset needs to be as large as possible. In this case inspection is carried out on the claims of one representative record from each family.

In this example search strategies provided a list of over 1,100 families; a member of each was inspected and characterised. At this stage any non-relevant families were removed, giving a final categorised set of 623 patent families

To ensure that any insights are accurate, after the data is exported, it is cleaned; all publications from the families are included, not just the one inspected, the categorisation of the representative member is used for all members of the family. This may introduce a certain amount of misrepresentation, as different family members may represent different aspects of the invention, however in this case the limitations are acceptable.

The data that has been extracted may contain errors and inaccuracies, plus information may have changed over the lifecycle of the records, such as the assignment of applications and patents between different entities. Most of the leading patent database providers clean their data and offer information on assignments and so the most up to date bibliographic and assignee information is readily available.

The 623 patent families in this example provided a list of over 6,000 individual publications. Records that may give a duplicate result when looking at numbers of applications or grants in the set, for example A3 search report publications, are removed.

Analysis

The analysis of the data can begin by a simple inspection of the dataset, however trends and insights are best observed by using graphical representations, as illustrated in Figure 3.4.1

Figure 3.4.1 – Breakdown of applications over time in the different sections relating to pregabalin.

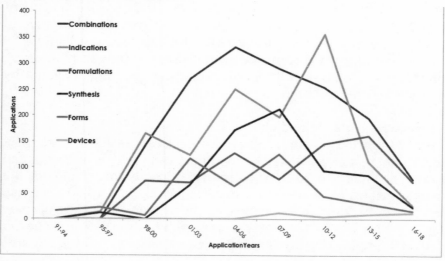

To start, a breakdown of the different sectors is extracted to see the level of activity by means of a count of the number of applications. This can then go further, by looking at application years, to give an idea of when the activity took place.

Immediately trends appear, which may not necessarily be surprising. Early on, when the drug is first developed, there are the applications relating to the drug form itself and to its synthesis, but then after around 1997 its use in combinations takes off as well as applications relating to its indications. The peak for combination applications occurs around 2004-2006, whereas for indications it is later, at around 2010-2012. All the numbers appear to drop off in later years; this is perhaps what would be expected in relation to a drug that is over 20 years old, but this also highlights a flaw in the data analysis. Due to the lag time of 18 months between filing applications and their publication, the data will be incomplete for 2017 and 2018.

There are a huge number of other representations of the data that can be used to gain other insights. A closer look at the inventors involved can reveal who is working in which areas, and with which organisations they are or have been associated with. Also, geographical representations can be used to understand where applications in each of the sectors are being filed or where they claim priority, which would indicate where the research and development was occurring (see Figure 3.4.2). Similarly, a look at where patents are granted can show where the related products are marketed.

Figure 3.4.2 – Overall look at which territories applications relating to pregabalin are filed

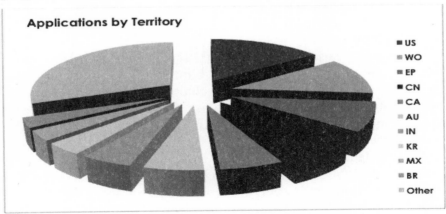

As the focus of this example was to show a technical study, another important tool would be to look at citation analysis. Patents that are frequently cited in other applications may be of particular importance in the area, or may be thought of as a standard in the field. In this case the majority of the top cited patents in the synthesis sector are in the name of Warner Lambert; the drug was developed by Parke-Davis, a subsidiary of Warner Lambert, and was first marketed by Pfizer after they acquired Warner Lambert in 2000.

Conclusions
The use of landscape studies looking at technical features is extremely versatile. As long as the initial searches are robust, and the data is collected and cleaned appropriately there is a vast amount of information that can be invaluable to R&D departments. The visualisation of the areas of existing innovation can be used to expand established technology sectors and explore potential new ones.

LANDSCAPE STUDY II – ELECTRIC VEHICLES

Objective
The subject matter for the second study was chosen, as it is currently at the cutting edge of technology in the automotive industry, and because of the increase in popularity of electric vehicles in recent years. Electric Vehicles (EV) are covered by a number of different technologies, which makes this subject more suitable to showcase a high-level corporate landscape analysis, which we are presenting in this example.

The objective of this study is to show general trends in this broad technology field, to identify the main players in the field, and give a geographical breakdown of filing and filing trends.

Methodology
For this study we used keyword-based strategies, covering basic terms like EV and electric vehicles, without limiting the search by specific classification headings. The search excluded the terminology covering hybrid vehicles in order to reduce noise. In order to focus the search to cover the most recent trends the search was limited to records with priority date within the last 5 years. The search was performed on a worldwide dataset, which resulted in over 35,000 patent families with over 62,000 publications. The search and analysis were performed in PatBase™ where the analytics tool offers a number of options for adjusting the analysis, which is helpful in the interpretation of the results. In this study we analysed both applications and granted patents as they offer different insights into the field.

Analysis

The number of patent applications per year in this technology field for the past five years is in steady growth, almost linearly. The number of filed patents in 2016 was over 12,000, with this trend we can expect that the global filing numbers will reach 15,000 per year by 2020. In the same time roughly half of these applications are reaching the granted stage.

The assignee analysis of figure 3.4.3 shows that the big automotive giants still hold the majority of the top positions, Toyota, Hyundai, Ford, Mitsubishi, Nissan, etc.

Figure 3.4.3 – Top 10 Assignees in the field of Electric Vehicles by number of applications, including a separate bar for number of grants.

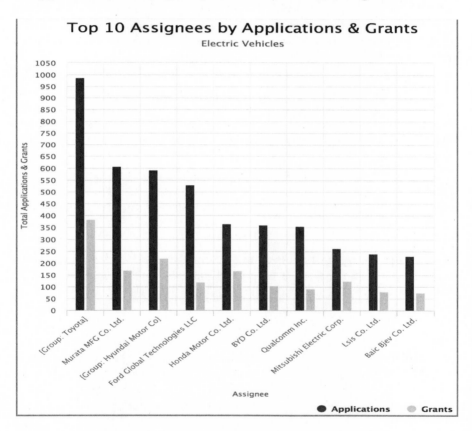

In the top ten, as may be expected, there are also some large electronic companies like Maurata MFG, Qualcomm and Siemens. It is also useful to see that there are some smaller companies active in the field of EV technology, namely BYD Co, Lsis Co, Baic Bjev and NTN Corp.

A similar study showed that Robert Bosch, Samsung and Sony hold nearly 900 relevant patents between them in the field of EV innovation, which place them in a strong position for the future, although they do not yet appear on the top 10 list.

The further analysis showed that there are a significant number of new companies that are entering this technology area, e.g. Thunder Power New Energy Vehicle Dev Co Ltd, Faraday & Future Inc, Chengdu Yajun New Energy Automotive Technology etc., the majority of them based in China. Although they may not be at the top of the assignee chart at the moment, it may be of interest to monitor their activities in the future.

To get a better insight into new companies entering the field, additional studies can be extended to give an idea of the importance of patents in the field. A score can be assigned to a particular patent depending on its value to the sector, for example based on the number of times it is cited. This weighting of the results can show that some larger companies may have large patent portfolios, consisting of low value patents, whereas newcomers may hold few, but high value, patents.

Looking now at the data in Figure 3.4.4 below representing the geographical breakdown, it appears that almost 66% of applications are filed in China, more than 32,000 in the past 5 years; second is USA with around 4,800 and third Japan with over 3,000 patent applications. The location of applications gives an idea of where R&D in the field is performed.

This order for the top territories is also kept when looking at the number of grants, which would indicate there is little difference between the location of technology development and the location the product is to be marketed.

Figure 3.4.4: Geographical heat map showing territories and numbers of applications in the field of Electric Vehicles

Top 50 Jurisdictions by Applications
Electric Vehicles

Conclusions

This is only a small example of the elements of a corporate landscape study that can be presented; a more in-depth analysis can be performed for a specific assignee/company, territories, specific technologies, classification headings etc. In recent years a lot of new analytic tools have appeared on the market that can create automated analyses of patent portfolios, however during the analysis it is important to be careful how we interpret the results as they heavily rely on the input and analytics options. Without specialist knowledge of data analysis the conclusions drawn may point to false trends.

References

http://markets.businessinsider.com/news/stocks/
some-branded-drugs-going-generic-in-2018-1013567302
https://www.dispensingdoctor.org/news/uk-patent-expiries-20172018/
https://www.medindia.net/drug-price/pregabalin.htm
http://www.medizzine.com/en/patients/drugs/P/pregabalin.php
https://www.pfizer.com/about/history/pfizer_warner_lambert
https://www.frontiersin.org/articles/10.3389/fbioe.2018.00084/full
http://www.energymanagermagazine.co.uk/EM-June-18.pdf -The Electric Vehicle Intellectual Property Report 2018; PatSnap

3.5

IP CONSIDERATIONS FOR IT INNOVATION

John Collins, Creation IP

Introduction

In our digital age, digital technology pervades all aspects of our lives, from simple everyday items such as washing machines, to mobile and landline telecommunications and complex networked computer systems, including the Internet. Digital technology is underpinned by hardware, but such hardware is most commonly programmed and hence controlled by software. For innovation involving software alone or both software and hardware, there are a number of facets of IP law that need to be considered and can assist in providing strong protection and add value for a digital technology-based business.

Some digital technology, such as artificial intelligence and neural networks, is considered a threat and a mystery by many people. In this chapter the various IP facets available for the protection of software-based innovation will be discussed to assist the reader in understanding how IP relates to this technology and to avoid overlooking potentially valuable IP assets.

THE IP OPTIONS

Those in the IT industry may be familiar with certain aspects of IP, but often such familiarity comes with misconceptions, such as "software is protected by copyright" and "software is not patentable". These misconceptions often result in lost opportunities to provide useful IP protection and bring value to the business.

The various options for IP protection for IT comprise, trade marks, copyright, patents and designs (registered and unregistered).

Trade Marks

Trade marks may be registered or unregistered. Unregistered trade marks may provide protection in countries having a common law system. Under this system, when a mark gains a sufficient reputation, the law of passing off or unfair competition can be used to enforce the unregistered mark against a third party to maintain the reputation of the mark owner. However, meeting the sufficient reputation standard can be onerous and registration of a trade mark is recommended.

A registered trade mark gives the owner of the registration the exclusive right to use the mark in connection with the goods and services for which it is registered. The owner of the registration can prevent third parties from using the same or similar mark for the same or similar goods or services without consent.

Trade marks are a form of IP that provide valuable commercial protection for an IT product. However, they focus on the branding aspects of the technology and not form or function of the IT product.

Copyright

A copyright work is created and hence an author acquires the right in an original work once the author creates the work in a tangible form of expression. Original works of authorship includes literary, dramatic, musical, and artistic works, such as poetry, novels, movies, songs, computer software, and architecture. A major limitation on copyright is that copyright protects only the original expression of ideas, and not the underlying ideas themselves. An 'expression' of an idea is the fixation of the idea in a tangible medium. In the IT field, a tangible medium includes digital storage and digital representation.

Although software is protected by copyright, to enforce a copyright it is necessary to initially prove that you have a copyright in a work and then to prove that the third party has copied the whole or a substantial part of your copyright work. Since the copyright work is the expression i.e. the code, copying of the code must be proven. Copyright will not provide protection against a third party copying the functionality of your software. This is illustrated well in a decision of the UK High Court in the Navitaire v Easyjet case[10] in which Easyjet created a new

---

10. NAVITAIRE INC (Claimant) v. EASYJET AIRLINE COMPANY and BULLETPROOF TECHNOLOGIES INC [2004] EWHC 1725 (Ch) (30 July 2004)

booking system based on the functionality of Navitaire's system and was considered not to infringe Navitaire's copyright in the software because the program's functional aspects and interfaces are not protected by copyright. It was held that writing original source code that results in a similar or an identical function to another program does not result in infringement of the copyright in that program.

Hence, copyright protection for software has a limited scope of protection and only covers copyright and hence it represents a no cost or low-cost IP right.

Patents

A patent protects an invention against being used by a third party for a period of up to 20 years from the filing date of the patent. The protected use includes use, distribution, importation, selling and keeping. A patentable invention is an invention in a field of technology. The contentious issue is whether or not software is a patentable invention. Even though software clearly is used in a technical field, not all software performs a new technical function or has some new technical effect, and hence not all software is patentable.

It is important for the IT industry to be aware that many patents are granted for software related inventions, even by one of the most restrictive patent offices, the UK Intellectual Property Office. The laws of what constitutes patentable software are complex and vary significantly in different countries. In Europe, software is deemed patentable if the functions performed by the software bring about a technical effect or solve a technical problem. The technical effect or problem can lie in the field of computer programming or IT in general. In the US, the test for patentable subject matter is whether the invention is not 'abstract'. This proving of a negative has challenged the legal system in the US and the exact parameters required for a software related invention to escape the abstract exclusion is not clear. Applying a European approach to defining a technical solution to a technical problem in US patents, is one approach to arguably meet the not abstract test.

Hence, a lot of software-based inventions are patentable, but not all and the details vary country by country. Legal guidance from an experienced patent attorney is required to steer through this legal minefield to identify if patent protection may be available and then to draft a patent specification that will provide the strongest chances of being approved by the patent offices of the countries in which patent protection is required. Patent protection, if available for the IT technology provides the strongest form of IP protection. It does however require significant investment and the granting process can take several years

Designs

Designs can be protected by way of unregistered design rights and registered designs.

Unregistered Designs

UK and EU unregistered design right, like copyright is created and hence an author acquires the right in an original work once the author creates the work in a design document or an article. The design must consist of the shape or configuration of the whole or part of an article. The design cannot be a method or principle of construction, surface decoration of an article, features of shape or configuration of an article which enable the article to fit another article to perform its function, or features that are dependent upon the appearance of another article of which the article is intended to form an integral part.

In the IT industry and particularly in the field of software, unregistered design right has limited applicability and hence value. However, it does represent a no cost or low-cost IP right.

Registered Designs

Most countries provide for the registration of designs. The details of the law in each country varies. However, in generality, registered designs protect features of the shape and configuration of a two or three-dimensional article. Design registration is available for new designs for a whole or part of an article. In some countries such as the EU and UK, design protection for graphical user interfaces and computer icons is available, even though the design may be ephemeral and produced only during the execution of software on a display of a device.

The registration of designs has the important advantages over unregistered design right, in that a registered design does not require any proof of entitlement or ownership, and it can protect surface decoration, which includes logos and graphical user interfaces. Further, the term or protection of a registered design can be up to 25 years with payment of five yearly renewal fees, in contrast with the term of UK unregistered designs of 15 years from creation or 10 years from first marketing, and only 3 years for EU unregistered designs.

The registration process is quick, typically taking weeks, and the costs are low relative to the patent process.

Registered design protection for aspects of a graphical user interface and for icons displayed by execution of software on a device therefore represents an often forgotten and underused aspect of IP protection in the IT industry. Registered designs can fill the gap left by copyright: the lack of protection for the function of the software. Often the appearance of the graphical user interface as a significant impact on the function of the software, or at least the function perceived by the user. The look and feel of a user interface of a device provided by a software implemented graphical user interface is an important part of the user perceived function of software executing on a device.

Hence, the fast and low-cost registered design protection option should be given serious consideration in an IP protection strategy.

CHALLENGES FOR THE IT INDUSTRY

Technology based on software has developed at an astonishing pace. New technologies, often considered futuristic only a few years ago, are readily available and often delivered in small handheld devices, such as mobile phones. The internet has developed and extended way beyond the traditional view of a network of computers to the internet enabling of everyday devices, such as refrigerators and domestic and industrial lighting, heating, etc., using the Internet of Things. Vehicles are now software controlled to a level that enables a range of functions from voice commands and self-parking to self-driving.

As new technologies emerge, the boundaries of IP protection are pushed, and IP law has to adapt.

Artificial Intelligence

One of the major facilitators of enhanced capabilities in software functionality is the field of Artificial Intelligence (AI). AI has been at the forefront of major technological advances in recent years and the field of AI is a broad field of computer science directed to enabling machines to behave and reason in an intelligent manner. Early AI systems were rule based deterministic systems and expert systems are an example of such a system in which rules are structured so that they could be navigated in order to arrive at a solution to a given problem or question.

Machine learning, including algorithms such as artificial neural networks and deep learning, is a move away from rule-based approaches towards approaches that can generalise and can learn from data.

AI can be considered at three different levels:

The algorithm level

At the algorithm level innovation and value lies deep within the steps or processes of the algorithm, without any consideration to the application of the algorithm to a particular technical problem, such as control of a function or the identification of data.

There is unlikely to be IP protection available for such fundamental processes. For example, the algorithm is unlikely to be expressed uniquely by a specific set of code and hence copyright would not protect the processes. There is no design output and hence design protection is not applicable. For patent protection, applying the approach of the US, a patent directed to the algorithm per se is likely to be considered to be unpatentable as merely being abstract. Applying the European approach, algorithms and mathematical methods as such are excluded from patentability as not providing a technical effect.

The Implementation level

At the implementation level, considerations are given to not just the processes of the algorithm, but to the interaction of the algorithm and software with the hardware, data or signals. Such processes may not be restricted to a particular application but can be widely applied to the processing of physical data and signals. For example, a machine learning algorithm may be applied to image processing in general, without restriction of the image processing field.

Since the algorithm is a more specific implementation involving real world data or signals, there may be some useful protection provided by copyright for a specific coded expression of the concept. There is no display output and hence design protection is not applicable. Patent protection may be available, since the algorithm may now be applied to a technical problem involving data or signals. When considering the US requirements, it can be argued that the concept is no longer merely abstract. When applying the European approach, it may be possible to identify a technical effect and a technical solution to a technical problem involving the use of the AI processes to process the data or signals.

The application level

At the application level, the AI processes are directed to specific processes in a specific field, such as medical image processing, or speech processing. At this level there is likely to be an IT product being marketed, either as a hardware and software combined product or solely as a software-based product.

All IP protection types of care are hence likely to apply at this level to the product. Trade marks can protect the brand. Copyright will protect the specific code expression. Registered design protection can be sought to protect aspects of the graphical user interface and icons displayed on the display of the user device. Patent protection may be available for a new solution to a specific technical problem in a specific technical field.

AI and patentability

Although AI is a fast-developing technology, the approach to the assessment of patentability for innovation harnessing AI is no different to any other software-based innovation. There are no special provisions or approaches and the general approach to IP has to be applied. Since it is unlikely that patent protection will be available for the core AI algorithm, the purpose and application of the AI algorithm must be considered to identify whether this lifts it above the abstract exclusion in the US, and for Europe, whether it enables the formulation of a technical problem addressed by the process which is solved by a technical effect of the process.

Hence, AI can just be considered a tool used within the software process executed by the hardware to provide a new and useful effect in technology and the approach to IP consideration is no different to any other software-based product.

There is, however, one interesting effect on IP protection for AI based patents brought about by the new EU General Data Protection Regulation (GDPR). An important aspect of patent protection is the ability to detect if a third party infringes the patent. The functions performed by an AI algorithm will typically be performed on a remote server or encoded in software in an encrypted manner such that the result of the AI process may not shed any light on how the AI process works. Hence, when investigating whether to enforce a patent against a third party being able to discover how the third party is carrying out their AI process is important. Where an AI based patented invention involves the processing of personal data, the GDPR can be a useful tool to assist in patent infringement determination.

The GDPR requires data controllers for a third party to disclose "meaningful information about the logic involved" when personal data is processed by the third party. The data controller is not required to provide the source code, or a complex explanation of the algorithms used. In the example given in the guidance documents, when a data controller uses credit scoring to assess and reject an individual's load application, the data controller is obliged to explain the scoring process and provide details of the main characteristics that helps them reach the decision.

Hence, the use of the GDPR legislation can be considered by the attorney drafting the patent to direct the scope of patent protection to include features that may be disclosed as a result of a GDPR request and the GDPR legislation can assist in the detection of infringement of AI based patents.

SUMMARY

Whether your business relates to applications for mobile phones, hand held electronic gadgets, computer games, financial systems, software or web-based services or any consumer product employing software functionality - all aspects of IP should be considered. In particular, when your IT product has a user interface, you should consider using the registered design process to provide fast and low-cost protection.

In addition, careful consideration needs to be given to seeking strong patent protection for the functional features of the IT product and experienced guidance sought to assist you.

3.6

START-UP BUSINESS: INVESTING IN AND CONTROLLING YOUR IP

Leah Grant, Impetus IP Limited

The Oxford Dictionary defines the term "Start-up" as *"the action or process of setting something in motion"*. So what is a Start-up business? A Start-up business is an exciting challenge of putting a business offering/idea into motion which in turn provides opportunities for creative thinking and role diversification when overcoming trials and tribulations along the way. So far this year just over 470,000 *(September 2018)* Start-up companies have been established in the UK alone. This is an encouraging amount of courageous entrepreneurs opting to take the plunge and start their own business each year. Apart from the date of incorporation, what sets a start-up business apart from an established SME?

Turbulent working environments, as seen in start-ups, tend to result in team members taking on responsibilities out of their usual remit and skill-set. Tight budgets, lack of funding or delivering on deadlines set by investors can put pressure on the team to cut corners. Ever-changing fast-paced working environments can promote creative thinking and innovation. It is vital that start-up businesses harness this creativity and ensure that commercial and IP opportunities aren't missed. This chapter outlines the importance of investing in IP from the outset and offers three different IP control solutions for new businesses.

Oxford Dictionary Quote:
https://en.oxforddictionaries.com/definition/start-up

Figure for Amount of Start-ups in 2018:
http://startupbritain.org/startup-tracker/

INITIAL IP INVESTMENT

Start-ups can either be constrained by tight budgets in the early stages of business or can benefit from an influx of capital from investors. Either financial situation should be very closely monitored to ensure the business's success once the initial "teething" period has passed and the business matures. Below are a few of the core areas that a start-up business should consider investing in from the outset.

Obtaining trademark rights for core house brand/business name
It is vital that the business's identity is protected to ensure that there is no confusion for customers either from competitors who provide similar products/service offerings or from businesses operating within a similar industry. Trademarks are an effective communication tool allowing customers viewing the trademark to know immediately who they are dealing with. A brand represents a business's reputation and can be a critical factor in determining whether a customer proceeds to engage in the business's services/purchase their products. The business may want to consider seeking advice from a Trademark Professional who will be able to advise the business on the most cost effective and broadest method of protection whilst also considering whether the brand will infringe upon anyone's prior rights. Additionally, advice can be found on your local Intellectual Property Office website.

Securing website domain(s)
Today more and more consumers look at a business's website before engaging their services/purchasing their products. The business's website can therefore be a very effective marketing tool. Domain names are easy to secure and maintain, a quick search can be completed online to see which domain names are available and simple steps can be taken to obtain the required domain. Purchasing multiple domains with different extensions should be considered as this provides the business with broader coverage.

Employing/partnering with an Intellectual Property Professional
Start-ups tend to have quick-paced working environments where new ideas grow and develop rapidly. It's vital that IP opportunities aren't missed as projects adapt, develop and take new directions. Hiring (or working with) an IP professional who is responsible for working within the team to draw out inventions and advising on the commercial value should not be overlooked. An IP professional will be able to advise whether ideas are worth investing further into in both money and time. They will also be able to assess whether the business has freedom to operate within the field of interest. An infringement law suit could dramatically knock back a start-up business, so this should be prevented at all costs.

Developing efficient processes that are fit for purpose
It is important not to restrict innovation by bogging the team down with too many processes that aren't fit for purpose. A process should be a streamlined method of capturing how a business task is completed identifying each stakeholder's role in the process. As previously mentioned team members within a start-up quite often take on responsibilities above and beyond their initial job description. Therefore, it's important to map out who does what within the business task to avoid confusion and unexpected delays. Start-ups may see a rapid increase in their staff headcount as the business grows and develops. Internal processes can help to facilitate the smooth introduction of new team members. In the early stages a process may adapt and change numerous times – this is ok, as the team trials and learns the best way of completing a task. However, the process shouldn't be changed too many times as this can cause confusion and resistance within the team.

CONTROLLING IP

It is vital to appreciate the fine line between the balance of freedom for innovation and creativity and the importance of the control and maintenance required on an IP portfolio. IP portfolios within start-up businesses can rapidly increase in size as the team's creative juices flow and new team members join with fresh ideas gained from previous experience within the industry/previous roles. Finding the balance between innovation and control is the sweet spot that is the foundation for a fruitful and successful business. Without innovation the business will not grow and adapt to the ever-changing market and without control the business could find themselves in a situation where their IP maintenance is jeopardised which could lead to last minute expensive fixes. There are many different models that start-up businesses could adopt in order to control their IP; it truly is a case of "one size does not fit all". It's important that businesses find a way of controlling their IP that fits into their way of working; they should not be controlled by their IP, they should control it. Below are three different methods of controlling IP which I have seen working in practice within start-up businesses that could be considered.

Option One: Utilising the services provided by an outside law firm

Working with an outside law firm could be a good place to start for a start-up business who may have little knowledge of IP including the different types, processes, filing systems and associated costs. A law firm would be easy for a start-up business to approach and engage, provided that there is no conflict of interest, as there are numerous IP law firms in the UK alone. A forward-thinking law firm would jump at the opportunity to work with an innovative start-up business.

Advantages
- There is an abundance of IP law firms in the UK alone.
- A large law firm will have Attorneys with knowledge in specific technology fields and will be able to match the business with a suitable professional.
- They could monitor deadlines etc. on their IP platform and notify the business when necessary.
- They will be able to advise on all legal matters and provide commercial advice.

Disadvantages
- They won't be on the ground working directly alongside the team drawing out inventions and capturing amendments to inventions and projects.
- This is not the most cost-effective option as the law firm will charge for their time on top of the official fees and will be difficult to budget as costs will vary depending on the amount of work instructed.
- Certain law firms can be quite rigid in their way of working, they may ask that the business works in line with their processes.

Option Two: Hiring an in-house IP Professional

Hiring an in-house IP Engineer/Patent Attorney with a commercial background could benefit a new business with either little knowledge (or a comprehensive knowledge) in IP. An in-house IP Professional could be instrumental in setting up internal IP processes, forming IP teams, capturing innovation, maintaining an IP portfolio and assisting and guiding commercial decisions. I have seen this method working in several different ways, a start-up business could consider this option in conjunction with Option One above or Option Three below.

Advantages
- They could work on the ground alongside the innovation team/ engineers drawing out inventions and attending project meetings to make sure that they are up to date on all innovations.
- They could draft and file IP applications.
- They could advise and enforce commercial decisions including selling/licencing IP.
- They could source an IP management system and build an IP team/delegate to a trusted IP partner to manage IP deadlines and handle IP prosecution under instruction.

Disadvantages
- The business may find it difficult to source an IP Engineer/Patent Attorney with a commercial background that has extensive knowledge of the industry/technology field of interest.
- The business will need to be willing to provide the IP Engineer/ Attorney with reasonable remuneration which will increase their overhead.
- The business may be required to pay the IP Engineer/Attorney in periods where there is little to no innovation if the situation should arise.

Option Three: Delegating to a trusted IP partner

Start-up businesses can be really creative with their IP management. Delegating to an equally creative trusted IP partner who is willing to tailor their services to the business's specific requirements would allow the business to adapt their IP processes as they mature. A flexible IP partner who has worked with businesses of many different sizes across a multitude of industries will also be able to offer their IP network of professionals when required to the business. This option could suit a start-up business that doesn't know specifically what they require or could suit a start-up business that is looking to delegate one or more specific areas.

Advantages
- Partners who provide flexible tailored services that fit in with existing processes or have the ability to help develop new or streamline existing processes.

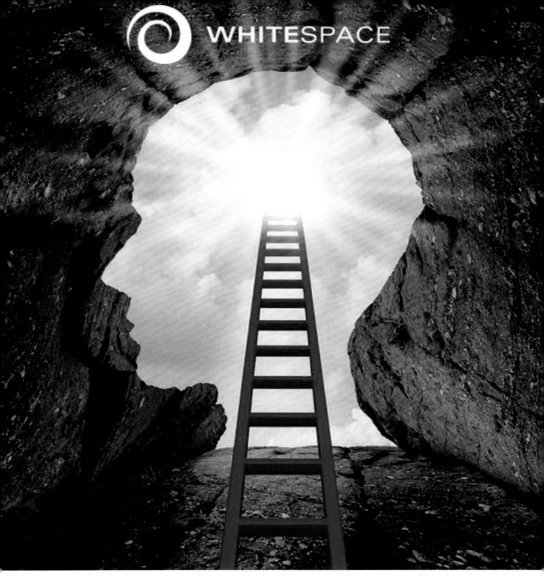

Our international network of professionals and clients invites you to 'beWhitespace' and experience this alm **of heightened consciousness and sustained well being.**

Karren Brooks, Whitespace founder

beWhitespace.com

patentGate

patentGate – patent information for your company

Patent monitoring with patentGate

patentGate helps you to monitor current intellectual property rights. Based on search profiles, technology trends, and inventions of competitors are retrieved. The patent documents can be distributed and evaluated. Company specific search fields, patent families, citations, and legal status information complete the database.

Reports and data sets: patent profile reports

Patent profile reports contain all recently published documents of the previous month covered by your search profile.
Every document includes bibliographic data and abstracts with a drawing. We can also provide patent data in other formats such as XML or CSV.

Legal status monitoring with patentGate

We monitor legal status changes of patent documents published in the patent registers of the authorities EPO, WIPO, DPMA, USPTO, JPO, SIPO as well as the INPADOC legal status database. You can choose whether you want to be informed about all or only about certain events and receive new results on the fly or as a spreadsheet or PDF document.

www.patentgate.de · patentGate GmbH · Hofgraben 5 · 98704 Ilmenau/Langewiesen · Germany

Brunel University London's Innovation support for SMEs goes beyond advice

Brunel Digital

Well established track record of carrying out world leading applied research in information and communication technologies (ICT). Working with industry, Brunel provides innovative, cost-effective solutions for real world problems in Big Data, Internet of Things, 5G, Distributed Ledgers, Verification and Validation, Machine Learning and AL.

Brunel Cleantech

Research focuses on technologies that dramatically reduce the use of natural resources and the impact on the environment, make significant energy efficiency improvements and cut or eliminate emissions, waste and cost. The outstanding facilities bridge the gap between fundamental laboratory scale research and full-scale industrial

Brunel Automotive

With world-class facilities and exceptional engineering capability, it delivers outstanding research through collaborative partnerships in automotive, thermal and materials engineering, electric machines and power electronics, design and mathematical modelling.

Environment, Health and Societies

Cutting edge science coupled with top-notch translated research into relevant and useful advice, products and services for end users, improving environmental quality, health and well-being both globally and locally. Core multidisciplinary research themes include Ageing studies, Biomedical Engineering, Environmental and Health, Health Economics, Synthetic Biology, Welfare, Health and Well-being.

Brunel holds an international character with worldwide industry collaborations. Its top notch research in the healthcare, automotive, clean tech and digital technologies makes it a unique collaborative partner for SMEs and beyond, willing to expand their product portfolio, by further developing their technologies/products and/or exploring new market potential.

Research Support and Development office

Technology transfer-business development managers, and/or academics could potentially approach companies for discussing collaborative opportunities. Applying for collaborative funding is supported by the RSDO and includes:

Funder	Project Type	Details and Participants
Innovate UK	Collaborative Research and Development	Funding to develop an innovative product, process or service. Industry-led. Can have multiple partners including academia, other businesses, & not for profit organisations etc.
	Knowledge Transfer Partnerships	The business must have a knowledge gap that can be filled by knowledge transfer from the university via the associate, to help the business innovate. Business led. A partnership between a university, business and an Associate.
European Commission	Research Innovation Action (RI)/ Innovation Action (IA)/ Coordination and Support Action (CSA)	Different actions including R&D, innovation activities and accompanying measures. RIA and IA require minimum 3 beneficiaries from 3 different EU Member States or H2020 associated countries, whereas CSA 1. Funding depends on the action
Global Challenges	Tackling challenges faced by developing countries	Development of enduring links between UK researchers and academic communities in developing countries. Participants include researchers, policy makers and practitioners as well as involvement from civil society and the private sector. Funding rates vary as defined in each specific call.
Newton Fund	Economic development & social welfare in developing countries	Strengthening partner country science and innovation capacity. At least one partner country from the OECD Development Assistance Committee list. Funding rates vary as defined in each specific call.
UK Research and Innovation	Various, across disciplines	Projects must push frontiers of human knowledge and understanding, and generate economic impact and social prosperity or social and cultural impact. Specific and open calls appear throughout each year across the Research Councils. Academic led, encouraging industry involvement.

Co-Innovate

Co-Innovate offers pragmatic support to help SMEs plan innovation projects, access specialist knowledge, skills and resources and help address the issue of access to funding and intellectual property. In doing so, it can stimulate, focus and accelerate innovation as well as de-risk it.

Specifically Co-Innovate provides:
- Innovation expertise
- Access to the right specialist skills; another significant barrier to innovation success
- Knowledge about and access to intellectual property resources
- Access to funding

This support enables creative collaborations to generate better ideas, new opportunities, as well as access to a large innovation 'ecosystem'.

HealthTec
at **Harwell**
MULTIDISCIPLINARY
INNOVATION

Space
at **Harwell**
MULTIDISCIPLINARY
INNOVATION

EnergyTec
at **Harwell**
MULTIDISCIPLINARY
INNOVATION

Harwell Campus
Brilliance Every Day

Aerial image of Harwell Campus

1. Public Health England
2. Medical Research Council
3. ISIS
4. Central Laser Facility
5. Research Complex at Harwell
6. HuSCO
7. Diamond Light Source
8. RAL Space
9. Satellite Applications Catapult
10. European Space Agency
11. Scientific Computing Data
12. Rutherford Appleton Laboratory
13. University Quarter
14. The Quad
15. Zephyr Building
16. Genesis Building
17. Residential Complex
18. Rosalind Franklin Institute
19. Faraday Institution

- Ability to draw upon IP Partner's network of trusted IP Professionals including Patent and Trademark Attorneys.
- Access to IP management systems, an IP Partner will be able to store the business's IP records on their own IP database or help the business source the best IP management product to suit their budget and business requirements.
- IP Partners will be able to offer advice on best/most cost-effective practices based on experience from working with current and previous clients.

Disadvantages
- This may not be as cost-effective as having an in-house IP team.
- May not have the ability work in-house alongside the team 5 days a week alike an in-house IP Professional. However, should this be required they may be able to accommodate for a short period of time initially until formal arrangements are made.

SUMMARY

A start-up business could consider the option of adopting and combining more than one of the above provided methods to ensure that their IP is controlled and maintained. In particularly productive periods when there is a lot of innovation and consequently an increased amount of IP activities the business could decide to outsource overflow work or an area of their IP activities to a trusted partner or law firm. To reiterate – "one size does not fit all". Above all, start-up businesses should feel that they are able to reach out to an IP Partner or Professional with any IP related query, be it regarding starting their IP portfolio, IP control solutions or sharing best practices. The IP industry is a support network of professionals with the ability to share their knowledge and network to ensure that innovation is supported and enriched.

PART FOUR
STIMULATING COMMERCIAL INNOVATION

4.1

R&D TAX CREDIT CLAIM BASED SHORT-TERM BRIDGE FINANCE FOR HIGH-TEC START-UPS

Dr Mark Graves, 1851 Technology Group, and Julia May, May Figures Ltd

EQUITY CROWDFUNDING AND THE RISE OF MULTI-ROUND LOWER VALUE FUNDRAISING STRATEGIES

The traditional route of financing an early stage technology company has been an initial round of friends and family financing, followed by (for those successful enough) more substantial venture capital funding, with government/bank loans aligned as available.

In recent years, however, there has been a growing trend towards Equity Crowdfunding of technology start-ups with a number of platforms such as Crowdcube, Syndicate Room, Seedrs & Angels Den offering self-certified high net worth individuals the ability to directly invest in technology start-ups companies from as little as a £10 per investment.

The exact process varies slightly from platform to platform but essentially companies produce an investment pitch summary, some basic financial projections and, in some cases, a promotional video/Q&A video interview, which are placed on the platform of the Equity Crowdfunding site and made viewable to registered users of the site.

There then follows a process typically lasting a couple of months, where investors can post questions to the site and founders of the company provide responses. During this process investors can invest up until either the time deadline or the maximum amount of funding required is reached. The platforms vary slightly in that on some it is necessary for the company to fully reach their target funding amount (although "overfunding" is allowed to a predefined maximum), whereas on others the company can close out the funding round even if they have not hit their defined target.

Everything considered, the effort required for companies to raise money in this way is generally significantly less onerous than that required of the traditional venture capital approach, where investors tend to be far more demanding in terms of their due diligence (that said, the online Q&A sessions can lead to some quite fiery exchanges – often triggered by investors questioning the valuation that founders place on their companies).

Although companies submit a certain amount of documentation on the website, potential investors may request more detailed pitch documentation in exchange for pledging to keep the additional documentation confidential. Despite this, companies need to be aware that the process is far more open than traditional VC funding pitches. For some companies, particularly those with a B2C product offering, the increased exposure and publicity can be a valuable addition to the funding and often such companies will provide small gifts/incentives to individual investors subject to SEIS/EIS rules.

As a result of the quick turnaround, large marketplace of investors, reduced due diligence, free advertising and simpler preparation required at the outset we are seeing many companies coming back for repeated rounds of Equity Crowdfunding investments, typically in the range of £150,000 to £1.5 million and delaying the move for institutional VC investment until they are more established and require significantly more funding. A number of smaller investment funds are also starting to co-invest alongside investment from individuals on the crowd funding platforms.

Consequently, many companies are increasingly following a fundraising profile of smaller and more frequent investment rounds, rather than an approach of entering a more significant investment round and managing the cash achieved as longer-term working capital.

Risks of Multi-round Low value Fundraising Strategy

Such a fundraising profile has significant advantages in terms of reduction of founders' equity dilution if managed correctly but conversely attracts significant risk if the timing/profile of the fundraising goes awry.

By taking a number of smaller fundraising rounds it is possible for a company to increase their valuation each round in response to some positive news. In the previous edition, "Developing a Patent Portfolio Strategy Optimised for Venture Capital Investment: Application to Early Stage Technology Start-ups" in Growing Business Innovation – Creating, Marketing and Monetising IP, edited by Jonathan Reuvid and published by Legend Press in 2017, we analysed how, for example, positive sentiment about a patent application can have a significant effect on the valuation of a company for a funding round. Equally other "good news" events such as a product launch, increased sales, an increased sales pipeline, and client endorsement, regulatory approval or large company partnership can all have significant potential to increase the valuation of a funding round.

Hence company founders can significantly reduce their overall equity dilution, by minimising the amount of funding they take at each funding round and increasing the valuation of the next funding round in response to some positive news event.

However, this approach is risky in that if there is a delay in the positive news event or worse still a delay in the fundraising round, then the company can experience very low cash reserves and may not be in a position to continue to pay its staff/development partners as planned. Opportunities may arise in the business that can't be taken up due to the aio or support such unforeseen opportunities.

LOAN FINANCING OPTIONS FOR EARLY STAGE TECHNOLOGY COMPANIES

It is in such circumstances that it would be ideal for a company to be able to access a short-term loan to tide the company over until the funding is received. However, it is rare for this to be possible since an early stage technology company does not typically have the assets or trading record against which a conventional financing company or bank would make a loan.

Usually such short-term loan financing is only provided as an emergency bridging loan by an institutional investor in the company and often this is constructed as a Convertible Loan Note. As such the loan can be converted to equity in the event of a default and usually at such a punitive valuation that the investors effectively end up owning the majority of the company with the founders being diluted out. Some might say this is appropriate given the failure to deliver against the loan, but for founders it is a devastating outcome.

Traditional short-term financing such as invoice factoring is only suitable for companies which have orders from established companies who are likely to pay the invoice. It is rare for early stage technology companies to have an order book and even if they had a significant order from one client it is likely to be against a new/unproved technology development and would hence be deemed too risky for most invoice factoring companies who want to see a regular and repeated payment of such invoices before advancing a loan backed against the invoice.

There are a growing number of web-based peer to peer loan offerings targeting small and relatively early stage companies. By far the biggest of these is Funding Circle which since 2010 has loaned £3.8 billion to 39,000 UK businesses. Whilst certainly more flexible in their lending than traditional high-street banks, such loan offerings are still targeted at "credit worthy" businesses and as such a pre-revenue, loss making technology start-up companies whose only source of income to date has been equity financing / director loans are almost certainly not going to be offered a short-term loan by even the more progressive P2P lending platforms.

Innovate UK Innovation Loans

The UK Government through Innovate UK have created a £50 million scheme of Innovation Loans as a pilot programme of loan competitions over two years to the end of 2019. These are aimed for innovations near to market, in contrast to grants which Innovate UK target at earlier stage, riskier innovations. They can also be used for late-stage research and development projects that have not yet reached the point of commercialisation.

An Innovation Loan may be offered where an SME can demonstrate they are suitable and eligible, specifically that they can afford the interest and repayments on the loan and then they cannot obtain finance from other sources such as banks and equity investors.

Under the Innovation Loan scheme companies can borrow between £100,000 and £1 million at an HM Treasury rate of interest, currently just 3.7% to over eligible project costs. The loan period is up to 10 years with the loan drawn down over a period of 3 years with security taken over assets purchased and intellectual property developed.

Whilst such a scheme, especially at such a low interest rate, should be very interesting to late stage, near-market companies with the ability to pay back the loan and a specific 2-3 year R&D project which needs funding, it is less suitable for earlier stage companies who essentially need shorter term loan financing to act as a bridging loan between equity investment rounds.

Patent Backed Lending

Often the only assets that an early stage technology company has are its patent portfolio, which is often work-in-progress. Whilst there are specialist lenders who will make loans backed by the patent portfolio the transactional costs of them undertaking the highly complex valuation of a patent portfolio are such that it is only viable for significant, long-term loans backed by an extensive patent portfolio likely to be of significant value.

Such cases are usually reserved for technology companies which have emerged from the proof of concept technology development phase and are now entering the scale-up / production stage.

For example, GIK Worldwide, a US technology company which developed a breakthrough technology in the field of video-conferencing, leveraged a patent loan in order to finance its business development. With the help of IP investment bank Taibbi Ltd, the company raised $17 million in debt provided by Pitney Bowes Capital based on an appraised value of $57 million for the collateral patents.

As well as patent loans there are other patent based financing instruments such as Patent Sale and Lease Back and Patent Securitisations but in common with Patent Loans, the high transaction cost means such financing is quite rare and only for companies with a large and valuable patent portfolio. More details can be found in "IP-backed Finance" by F Munari, C Odasso and L Toschi in "The Economic Valuation of Patents, Methods and Applications", Cheltenham, Edward, Elgar.

R&D Claim Backed Loans

In many cases an early stage technology company will have invested significantly in R&D and hence be anticipating an R&D tax credit claim at the end of their accounting period, which for a loss-making company can generate a cash refund available to cover any costs in the business.

Unfortunately, the company may be several months from their accounting year end, although they may be able to bring that forward which would accelerate the claim. Once at the year end, there can be a delay on the production of the accounts/tax claim. Once filed, HMRC process the majority of SME R&D Tax Credit claims within 28 days although during busy periods this may not be met.

For RDEC/Large claims (applicable not only to large companies but also to SME's whose projects have received notified state aid grant funding or been subcontracted from Large clients) the HMRC review is not obligatory for up to 18 months. Although in our experience HMRC have not been known to take this long, claims can still take several months to clear depending on HMRC resources. All of this presents a significant delay on expenditure being reimbursed under the scheme.

Another aspect to making an R&D tax credit is that it is a requirement of the R&D Tax Credit legislation that the company is a going concern at the time the claim is filed, and at the time it is paid out. HMRC take the view that this is calculated without taking into account the R&D refund. This can leave some companies in a "catch22 situation" where they would be solvent but for the absence of the tax refund. HMRC will undertake credit checks prior to paying out claims, to identify that the company remains a going concern.

In order to help early stage companies cope with these delays in receiving their R&D Tax Credits claims, there is an emerging field of loan financing whereby providers are making loans to companies secured on their future R&D Tax Credit claim(s).

It is early days in this industry and the handful of companies offering services in this area vary enormously in the terms of their financing with different approaches to the absolute amount of the loan, the amount of the loan relative to the R&D claim, setup fee, interest rates, duration of the loan, whether they insist on a personal director guarantee, default conditions in the event that the R&D claim is rejected by HMRC and any appeal is lost etc.

However, in summary, the loan is typically linked to an R&D Tax Credit Advisor identifying the potential value of the R&D claim and then the company receiving a % of that amount as a loan as effectively an upfront advance on the future pay-out of the R&D claim by HMRC.

For early stage technology companies who have undertaken R&D qualifying activities and are expecting an R&D Tax Credit claim to pay out in the future, managing their cash flow and fundraising timing profile alongside their R&D Tax Credit claim and securing a planned R&D Tax Credit loan as part of a fundraising profile can provide a very useful means to bridge between equity fundraising rounds, enabling founders to reduce dilution by increasing valuations between more frequent, smaller fundraising rounds.

Taking real-life case studies as examples gives an insight into how this new form of financing can help early stage technology companies.

Case Study 1: Emergency Loan following Investment Round collapse

Our client, a software development company developing next generation web searching tools was suddenly let down by an investor just prior to an investment round.

In order to enable them time to regroup and prepare a new investment round, working in partnership with their accountants and R&D Tax Credit Advisors we devised a loan strategy comprising:

- An immediate same day loan to pay the month end wages bill
- Evaluation of the working cash flow requirements over the next 2 months
- A shortening of their accounting year end
- Immediate preparation and filing of an R&D tax credit claim for the shortened accounting period
- Payment of a loan representing 75% of the expected R&D claim in 4 weekly drawdowns repaid when the R&D claim paid out

Case Study 2: Planned Loan to increase fundraising valuation

Our client, a developer of an e-commerce comparison website had been experimenting with advanced machine learning algorithms.

Although they had offers of VC funding, they believed they would achieve a higher valuation if they had time to experiment and test out these advanced machine learning algorithms on their data sets since a positive outcome of the machine learning experiment would de-risk the investment for the VC.

We undertook an analysis of their future R&D expenditure, their likely R&D claim rebate and made a loan enabling the client to focus on their development work and delay an investment round until a stage where they could secure a higher valuation.

4.2

SME: UNIVERSITY COLLABORATION

A DOORWAY INTO AN OPPORTUNITY-RICH INNOVATION ENVIRONMENT

Ian Ferris, Dr. Averil Horton, Eleftheria Ledaki,
Brunel University, London

SMEs have been widely encouraged to adopt innovation as a growth mechanism; however, research into innovation success shows that for SMEs especially, innovation is often fraught with a variety of risks and challenges.

Picture the following; you are an SME and have identified a market opportunity or perhaps you want to develop a new product or service. Maybe you simply have some great technology ideas that you feel could be developed into a new commercial proposition. You are aware that innovation has some risks and that to accomplish your goals you may need access to some specialised skills or expertise. It could be that you want to find some grant funding to help finance the activity, or some expert guidance to help turn your ambitions into a practical action plan.

Imagine then, having available to you one of the UK's largest innovation resources to help you accomplish your goals, where access to specialised expertise, knowledge and funding opportunities is possible, and importantly, a resource where commercial collaboration with SMEs is roundly welcomed.

Surprisingly to many SMEs, that is just what is possible today via an increasing number of innovation support initiatives operating from UK universities seeking to connect, collaborate and innovate with SMEs.

Universities are a well-established point on the UK innovation landscape. Larger corporations have long understood and benefitted from this, but for SMEs, collaboration with universities is a daunting proposition: it shouldn't be. The benefits for SMEs of working with a university on their innovation activity are potentially substantial, if they can find a way of unlocking that potential.

RELEASING THE VALUE 'LOCKED UP' IN UNIVERSITIES AND SMES – THREE MECHANISMS TO STIMULATE INNOVATION

In practice, three broad types of innovation support can be achieved through universities like Brunel. The first type; *'contract research'* is largely transactional in nature and typically sees an academic or university facility funded to undertake a specific task on behalf of an organisation.

The second type, centres on the commercialisation of research outputs. Here, ideas and intellectual property, derived primarily from university research, follow a structured path of development, enabled and developed with academic involvement through a number of structured stages towards commercialisation. In this model, universities will often seek out external organisations, SMEs included, with whom to collaborate on a specific commercialisation project.

The third type of innovation is most often involving SMEs and sees an SME seeking support from the university to help them exploit an opportunity they themselves have identified, a new gap in the market or the exploitation of an emerging trend etc. The specialised support in this case could focus on the development of a feasible commercial 'solution', a new product, service, process and so on.

For recognising the varied development challenge, timeframes, resource and expertise that each type of innovation requires, Brunel University has developed and made available to SMEs, a variety of support mechanisms and approaches to deal with each.

Commercialising university research – Helping SMEs cross the *"University Ditch of Death"*

A closer look at the second type of innovation that could involve SMEs, that centres on developing research coming out of the university, reveals some specific challenges that need to be addressed. The starting point for this type of innovation is just that – *university research output* – whether a clear invention, some intellectual property or simply an idea. It is not a well-defined commercial proposition simply requiring development, the output will be highly under-developed in terms of potential industrial application.

In an ideal world, a large external investment would provide the funding required for development of the research output into a fully functional, commercial product, prior to a subsequent commercial world journey over the well-known *Valley of Death*. Of course, this is rarely, if ever, the case and in reality, there is a large gap between the university *research output* and the *industrial demonstrator* that is required to generate confidence in the technology and therefore the required external funding and investment; the gap is the *University Ditch of Death*. This gap covers proof of principle, market validation, technical and business development, and production of an industrial demonstrator. Crossing the *Ditch* is difficult and so frustratingly slow that it risks the credibility of the commercialisation potential of the technology. Very many tranches of funding are required, usually only available in very small batches and often with long gaps between. For an industrial technology, crossing the *University Ditch of Death* typically takes more than 5 years, more than £1m, and a significant team, most of whom need to be from outside the university.

So why is commercialisation such a lengthy, and bumpy, ride? Simply because Research Council funding does not cover post-research development and neither do investors fund it. However, there are potentially two fundamental structures on each side of the *Ditch of Death*, **Impact Acceleration Account** (IAA) funding and **Innovate UK funding**, which can help. IAA funding, a springboard to start the process off, is provided by some research councils to accelerate the impact of research and can enable *proof of principle* demonstration of a research output. At the other end, there is a jetty reaching out to help - Innovate UK Funding – to enable the production of an industrial demonstrator, the *proof of concept*. The IAA springboard and Innovate UK jetty are helpful but the predicament is how we move from one to the other.

What is needed in between these two, crossing the *Ditch*, is a two-stage process. Firstly, *market validation* - understanding the potential industrial need, the industrial problem it may solve, appropriate routes to market, and of course who would be willing to pay for it. Market validation often concludes that the potential application is not quite the same as was originally envisaged; it also helps to define what the industrial demonstrator needs to demonstrate - and to whom. Secondly, *technical & business development*, guided by the market validation results; the *technical* development to ensure the technical benefits serve the identified industrial needs, and the *business* development to confirm the value proposition, clarify the economics, and determine the appropriate route to market and commercial vehicle.

These two stages can be envisaged as moveable pontoons over the *"Ditch of Death"* and working models exist for both – the **Innovation to Commercialisation of University Research** (ICURe) programme for market validation and the Research Council funded **Innovation and Knowledge Centres** (IKCs) for the technical and business development. ICuRe provides both process and funding for intensive market validation and something similar is being developed by the technology broker InPart. IKCs although currently only for 'flag waving' technologies such as synthetic biology and photonics, provide a model for the technical and business development process – mentoring, facilities and funding.

The final 'tweak' required to make it across the *University Ditch of Death* is to recognise that it is the university that is responsible for driving the whole process and when supported by risk-appropriate funding which the university can often help acquire, will smooth the voyage over the ditch and enable universities to bring their technologies through to early application.

The overall objective is to partner with external organisations, SMEs included, to progress the commercialisation of university research to full industry buy-in and funding – for both 'really new' industrial technologies and for incremental ones. A clear process, high risk public funding, built in stage gates, and meeting industrial pull is the only way to ensure more, better, and faster (incremental) industrial innovation.

SME INNOVATION SUPPORT THAT GOES BEYOND ADVICE

The third type of innovation support provided by universities deals with support in developing new products, services and processes as a direct response to market opportunities or initial business ideas identified by the SME themselves. SMEs often focus on this sort of innovation activity as it builds on their market knowledge and experience. However research by the EU amongst others has identified a number of innovation barriers encountered by SMEs.

In recognition of this, Brunel University London, with co-funding from the ERDF London programme, launched their SME innovation support programme, 'Co-Innovate'. Co-Innovate is a support platform, that recognises the variety and individual needs of SMEs and focuses on addressing some key innovation barriers as a way of helping them progress their innovation ambitions, for example:

- **Limited in-house experience of innovation** – Because of the variety of available innovation theories, methodologies, tools and techniques, understanding which method, approach, strategy etc. is right for a given situation is a challenge and a potential risk. Smaller businesses especially tend not to have internal innovation specialists, further compounding the issue of developing the right approach. Through their experienced Innovation Directors, Co-Innovate performs an individual diagnostic with each SME client. This activity defines an 'Innovation Roadmap' that outlines the project strategy, supporting action plans and initiatives to close any capability gap, either from within university resources or externally. This sort of collaborative planning session, often including academic experts, is key to what follows and importantly, can consolidate vague or unclear ideas into something more focused, practical and actionable.

- **Limited access to the right specialist skills, knowledge and expertise** – Innovation projects usually require a range of specialised skills and knowledge, often outside the SME's core competencies. With over 1,200 academics operating across 30 discipline areas including; engineering, electronics, design, digital, computer science, business, bio-engineering, Brunel University, like other universities, offers access to a very wide range of high-level expertise and specialist knowledge relevant to commercially focused innovation and, importantly, in one place.

- **Lack of knowledge about and access to intellectual property** – As discussed earlier, innovation in SMEs often centres on exploiting opportunities identified by the business themselves, generating new solutions and intellectual property, *during* the innovation project. Culturally, academics have an openness to collaboration, high levels of creativity and willingness to share ideas, making them well-suited to projects aiming to generate novel solutions and IP. Practical agreements to ensure fair IP ownership rights generated within projects, are always put in place at the outset of collaborative activity to encourage collaboration.

- **Access to funding** – Academic involvement in an innovation support project usually requires funding and, on a larger scale project costs can be significant. Co-Innovate addresses this by encouraging joint applications to funding bodies such as Innovate UK. There is a belief in many SMEs that the funding application process is prohibitively complex, a perceptual barrier that prevents the exploitation of these funding opportunities.

Co-Innovate works with SMEs to facilitate the development of grant applications that include academics, whose subsequent involvement would be enabled by any funds secured. To help further, Brunel University has initiated their own 'Innovation Vouchers' scheme to build initial momentum by funding the early stages of selected collaborations. The funding involved is modest but so is the application process; in practice, this is an effective way to stimulate new SME-academic partnerships.

Programmes like Co-Innovate offer pragmatic support to help SMEs plan innovation projects, access specialist knowledge, skills and resources and help address the issue of access to funding and intellectual property. For the SME willing to invest time and effort in collaborating with a university, the benefits can go far beyond technical advice and access to specialist resources. The real win for an SME comes when they view the university as part of their own 'innovation system' and through the relationship, adopt new ways of working, with an emphasis on collaboration, co-creation and openness to sharing ideas. As a result, previously unforeseen benefits often emerge:

- **Collaboration with a university can be a 'force multiplier'** – Innovation is dependent on creativity and knowledge to generate and shape ideas into solutions, if this creativity and knowledge comes solely from within the SMEs own organisation, it can be a limitation. Leveraging value from a much larger resource simply makes sense for a smaller organisation, especially if this can be realised in a relatively low-risk manner.
- **Creative-collaboration can lead to more and better ideas, new opportunities** – Working with independently-minded academics to identify and generate new ideas, concepts and opportunities, can result in a significantly better commercial propositions, intellectual property and also organisational learning for even the smallest SME.
- **Access to a large 'Innovation Eco-System'** – the scale and diversity of universities can make them difficult to navigate but this also provides an opportunity. Having visibility of emerging research in specialist knowledge areas, and the chance to interact with the academics generating those research outputs, could be competitively advantageous as well as present an advanced perspective on new commercial opportunities. Universities themselves operate within a much larger network of organisations and connections and this offers many possibilities

for collaborating SMEs to extend their own networks into new directions and with that, gain visibility of new opportunities.

Universities and SMEs are both critical to the UK economy but today, can have a rather distant relationship. From the outside, universities to some may seem to lack commercial relevance, or appear challenging to engage with. Brunel University's support initiatives described here along with similar schemes operating in other universities, can provide a doorway into what is, in reality, a dynamic, knowledge-rich environment that can inspire, stimulate and support innovation success. All that needed is the willingness to go through that doorway and unlock that value.

Reference to EU research – Barriers to Innovation in SMEs: Can the Internationalization of R&D Mitigate Their Effects? Tiwari and Buse, 2007

4.3

CROSS-DISCIPLINARY INNOVATION THROUGH CLUSTERS

Barbara Ghinelli, Harwell Science & Innovation Campus

We live in an era of explosive technological change, coupled with mounting global economic and societal challenges to which technology can offer at least a partial solution. Keeping track of technology development, even within a single discipline, is far from easy. Understanding what is available in disciplines other than your own is that much harder. Yet it is well known that innovation thrives when people from different backgrounds mix, particularly if they are focused on a common problem.

At the Harwell Science & Innovation Campus, we are constructing an ecosystem that promotes cross-disciplinary working and information exchange. This task is helped by the fact that Harwell hosts several large facilities that are used by researchers across a broad spectrum of research and development. Thus, there is a constant throughput of people from different fields that use these facilities, and a local community that reflects this wide range of interests.

The Harwell Campus has been developed around the Rutherford Appleton Laboratory (RAL), a UK National Laboratory that is responsible, either solely or in partnership, for large "open access" scientific facilities such as the Diamond Light Source (and cryo-EM facility), the ISIS neutron and muon spallation source, the Central Laser Facility and the Research Complex @ Harwell. RAL is part of the Science & Technology Facilities Council (STFC), which is one of the seven main UK Research

Councils now under the umbrella of UK Research & Innovation (UKRI) with an annual budget of £6 billion.

The other major historical activity at Harwell was conducted by the UK Atomic Energy Authority, but as nuclear research activities transferred to other sites more suited to the changing nuclear environment, the land occupied by UKAEA became free. The UK Government took the decision about a decade ago to establish the Harwell Science & Innovation Campus on the former UKAEA site to encourage closer contact between industry and the research base, promoting technology transfer and economic development. The Campus is owned and operated by a 50:50 public-private Joint Venture made up of STFC, the UK Atomic Energy Authority and a private sector developer, Harwell Oxford Partners with U+iplc, to proactively help accelerate the commercial development of the site.

Over the past decade, the range of activities on the Campus has grown. The European Space Agency has established its first UK facility at Harwell (the European Centre for Space Applications & Telecommunications – ECSAT), and this has been joined by the Satellite Applications Catapult. These new Space-focussed organisations add to the pre-existing RAL Space, which is part of STFC. More recent additions include the Rosalind Franklin Institute, a new national institute, announced in 2017 by the UK government with a £103m grant, dedicated to bringing about transformative changes in life science through interdisciplinary research and technology development alongside engineering & physical sciences; and the Faraday Institution headquarters, dedicated to advanced battery research to ensure that the UK remains a leader in the field.

Augmenting the public-sector organizations is a growing list of commercial companies, ranging from large corporates that have established a presence at Harwell to develop synergies with the other activities on the site, to SME's and start-ups who see it as an ideal place to develop and grow. Altogether there are now over 5,500 people working in more than 200 organizations at Harwell, and these numbers continue to grow on the back of an ambitious building programme for new working and research space, together with further amenities and residential accommodation thereby creating a broad science & innovation community rather than a simple business park.

However, co-locating individuals and organizations is just the start. To fully benefit from the juxtaposition of knowledge and skills, we need to establish an environment where people are encouraged to interact and create the spark of innovation; and we also need to build cultural bridges that help people from different fields and different backgrounds (for example, academic researchers and industry) to appreciate the context in which each operates to be able to work together more effectively.

This is very much a work in progress, but in the remainder of this chapter I will discuss the steps we have taken thus far to try to create an ideal innovation ecosystem.

THE ROLE OF CLUSTERS IN THE DVELOPMENT OF HARWELL

The development of Harwell has been greatly accelerated by the establishment of Clusters in key thematic areas which reflect the strengths of Harwell and the potential for economic growth and societal benefit.

The first of these was the Space Cluster, motivated by the need to create an ecosystem around the newly established ESA ECSAT centre, to ensure that the UK benefitted from the ESA facility and the investment in it. This Space Cluster has grown from two organizations (ECSAT and RAL Space) to more than 80 in less than a decade, including commercial companies across the full spectrum of size and competences. The staff count in the Space Cluster is increasing at about 13% per annum every year.

Further Clusters have been established in Healthcare Technology / Life Sciences (HealthTec; 2016) and Energy (EnergyTec; 2018). HealthTec / Life Sciences currently encompasses about 50 organizations, either on the Harwell Campus or closely networked to it; whilst EnergyTec currently includes over 20 organizations.

While the Clusters provide an identity and nucleating theme, in practice many organizations are active in more than one of these thematic areas, or at the intersection of the disciplinary boundaries. These interdisciplinary interests are often stimulated by contacts made at Harwell networking events, and very much reflects the multidisciplinary ethos of the Campus that we are striving to develop further.

In the innovation context, the term 'Cluster' can be used to describe any, usually geographically co-located, set of organizations that have some common interests and objectives; or more simply, a Cluster exists when it becomes easy to move jobs without moving homes! In the case of Harwell, we think of the term as representative of a supportive ecosystem that drives win-win benefits for its component organizations. Although the nucleus of each Cluster is at Harwell, they are intentionally outward-looking and open to regional, national and international partnerships that serve the innovation agenda.

The benefits of being part of a Harwell Cluster
Benefits include:

- *Ease of collaboration*: Inter-company relationships are proactively fostered by the Cluster management and frequent themed networking events, so that when opportunities for collaboration arise the underlying relationships between companies are already in place, allowing them to be responsive and focus on goals and delivery. Collaboration allows companies to share risk, and develop more competitive propositions by combining expertise.

- *Integration into the research base*: As part of a Cluster, companies at Harwell have ready access to the considerable "open access" research facilities and expertise on the site, and in its wider national and international networks. Thus, companies have access to the latest technological developments together with experts that can support their commercialisation.

- *Strong commercial engagement*: As well as tapping in to the research base, the Harwell Clusters have a critical mass which makes it much easier, as an entity, to engage with companies and commercial interests elsewhere. This is particularly valuable to small companies who might otherwise struggle to be heard. The Harwell brand is thus an asset in its own right.

- *Mobile skilled workforce*: The Harwell workforce is a pool of highly skilled individuals from which companies on site can identify and attract the right individuals in a timely manner, alongside the flexibility to engage in short term or exploratory activities.

- *National & International Links*: Because of its critical mass and engagement in a range of international R&D activities, Harwell is well networked both nationally and internationally, allowing Cluster companies to leverage new relationships relatively easily.

- *Access to facilities*: Harwell is facility rich in terms of the large "open access" national and international facilities it hosts. Being part of the Campus community and its clusters makes it much easier for companies to know what is available, how individual facilities can be of use to them, and have access to the expertise required to exploit the results. They can also use the expertise on site to develop new facilities that they need for their business, perhaps sharing cost and risk with others in the Cluster.

All this adds up to an ecosystem that allows companies and other organizations to respond to opportunities in an agile and effective manner, thus increasing competitiveness.

The management and structure of clusters

However, while the advantages of being part of a Harwell cluster community are clear, realising these benefits requires a degree of pro-active management, particularly in the initial development of a cluster to kick-start relationships. To this end, each Cluster has a dedicated manager and its own 'Development Group' which meets regularly and is populated by representatives of cluster organizations on and off Campus. The development groups work in a collegiate manner to share opportunities, develop Cluster-wide initiatives and to help create an enabling environment that allows component organizations to achieve their aims.

We have also created a Cluster Steering Board that sits alongside the Cluster Development Groups. The Steering Board consists of representatives from the major Cluster stakeholders, including facility directors, and includes representatives of local network and regional organizations such as the Oxford Local Enterprise Partnership, a voluntary partnership between local authorities and business. This wider membership is part of the outward-looking ethos of the Campus, and the desire to form strong, mutually beneficial links with the many centres of expertise throughout Oxfordshire, the Oxford-Cambridge-London triangle, and beyond.

This governance structure is designed to be open, transparent and neutral, and to encourage Cluster organizations to find novel ways to collaborate and exchange information to mutual benefit. On the ground, these aims are supported by regular networking events, both at Campus and Cluster level. The HealthTec / Life Sciences Cluster has also instigated a small grant scheme to promote new collaborations between industry and public-sector Campus organizations. This scheme, funded by STFC and the Rosalind Franklin Institute, has been enthusiastically received by industry, and has succeeded in raising awareness of what Campus organizations can offer, leading to several new long-term collaborations; in some cases, these new relationships have been a significant factor in encouraging companies to locate on the Campus. Similar schemes are now planned for the other Clusters.

The growth in collaboration with industry is also creating greater demand for time on the Harwell large facilities. Plans for ongoing facility development are taking this additional demand into account, creating a positive feedback in terms of growing the capabilities of the research infrastructure. An excellent example is the new Electron Bio-Imaging Centre (eBIC) recently opened by the Diamond Light Source. A collaboration between Diamond Light Source and Thermo Fisher, this is the first high-end cryo-electron microscope facilities worldwide to be embedded alongside a synchrotron, with the generous financial support of both Johnson Matthey and Rolls Royce. It is an integrated facility for structural biology that will accelerate R&D for both industrial and academic users, and is a significant development for the Harwell HealthTec / Life Sciences Cluster.

A further factor in the growth of Harwell is the quality and suitability of the built environment. The private sector partner in the Harwell Campus Joint Venture is actively involved in the governance structure of the Clusters and other Campus activities, and thus directly engaged with the aspirations of Campus organizations. The Campus is large – over 700 acres – with an ambitious Master Plan to create 4.8 million square feet of new working and research space at an attractive range of price points. Thus, not only do companies and other campus organizations have access to skills, expertise and research facilities, but also the opportunity to create an ideal working environment for their needs within a growing science & innovation community.

Alongside working space, the Campus development plans include leisure and service amenities, and also affordable housing. This creates the possibility of the Campus itself becoming a tool for innovation, by developing as a 'living laboratory'. As a location and a community, Harwell Campus exemplifies many of the challenges faced by wider society in terms of creating an efficient and sustainable environment, and a thriving community rather than a simple business park. We can exploit the broad platform of expertise already co-located at Harwell to focus on developing innovative solutions to societal challenges that work in a real-world environment. In this way, the Campus will become a vehicle to demonstrate and refine solutions that can then, with confidence, be rolled out to a wider market.

To illustrate this, the large facilities on the Campus are very power-hungry. They would thus be an excellent test bed for solutions that re-cycle waste heat to the benefit of other residents. Similarly, the Campus is sufficiently large that transportation is an issue, both internally and between the Campus and other centres in the region, creating opportunities to develop and trial novel transport solutions. These innovations will be combined with 'smart housing' that is integrated into the energy, transport and environmental infrastructure to contribute to a better quality of life for residents and minimise their environmental impact.

Harwell Campus is already a fun, exciting and stimulating place to work and live. The breadth and depth of the "open access" facilities and opportunities at the Campus create a special environment for innovation, while its mixed-use nature could allow it to become an effective testbed for future environmentally friendly solutions to infrastructural challenges such as energy, transport and the general quality of life. By working in partnership at all levels, we want to build on the strong foundations already established to create an ecosystem that supports sustainable economic growth and the long term societal benefits which that brings to all members of the Harwell Science & Innovation Community as well as more broadly to UK plc.

4.4

ADAPTING DEFENCE TECHNOLOGY TO BUSINESS ENTERPRISE

Paddy Bradley, Swindon and Wiltshire Local Enterprise Partnership

On the 23 January 2017, the Government released for consultation its Green Paper, "Building our Industrial Strategy". The consultation sought responses on a range of issues including views on industrial sectors and the structures and processes necessary to enable the UK to be a competitive and successful global innovator and trader. In addition, areas of the country were asked to identify what made them special and distinctive and which would warrant investment to produce world class products and process performance. The 38 local enterprise partnerships in England singularly, and in some cases collaboratively, responded with enthusiasm to describe their versions of potential local industrial strategies.

In its response, the Swindon and Wiltshire Local Enterprise Partnership (LEP) identified the outstanding features of the area's economy and focussed on those future-oriented opportunities with excellent scope for expansion. Amongst those economically powerful combinations was the location of major defence technology expertise and the increasingly productive routes to commercially successful enterprises.

The Swindon and Wiltshire LEP is at the heart of a thriving defence science and security technology cluster in central southern England and is home to a range of leading companies including QinetiQ, Porton Biopharma, and Chemring Countermeasures, and also major research led organisations such as Defence Science and Technology Laboratory (DSTL) and Public Health England (PHE). Wiltshire is home to a quarter of the British Army and has major assets in defence and security technologies, including the Chemical Biological and Radiological research and development capability at Porton and through DSTL and the Ministry of Defence (MoD) site at Lyneham, which hosts the Defence College of Technical Training (DCTT), which includes the Defence School of Electronic and Mechanical Engineering. The MoD site at Boscombe Down is an established centre of excellence for aerospace defence and security technology, hosting 2000+ staff.

DSTL manages £380 million per annum of UK Government funding on science and technology projects. The new Porton Science Park, forming part of a wider campus, is a unique opportunity offering a state of the art 10 hectare defence and security research and development facility. Porton carries out research to ensure that the UK's military and wider public benefit from the latest technical and scientific developments. The UK Government is investing £115 million in developing new facilities at Porton, which will bring 650 new jobs to the area. Porton has close links to PHE, world leaders in high quality microbiological research and testing, and DSTL, specialising in development of effective countermeasures against chemical and biological events, and Porton Biopharma Limited, established in 2015 to commercialise research outputs into pharmaceutical development and manufacturing. Recently, Boeing Defence UK (BDUK) selected Boscombe Down as its preferred choice for its new UK headquarters, delivering 1,500 jobs and a multi-million pound investment. It will work with QinetiQ on defence-related aerospace activity. The LEP sees this as the first step in the development of a commercial defence technology site in the south of Wiltshire.

Swindon and Wiltshire is already home to a wide range of world class advanced engineering companies, including Honda, which has recently invested £250m in its plant at Swindon and has employment levels back above pre-crash numbers. Dyson, one of the UK's leading high technology engineering companies and the country's largest investor in robotics, is creating a new campus at the Hullavington Airfield, near Malmesbury, increasing its footprint in the UK by ten-fold. This is in addition to its £560m commitment to its existing campus at Malmesbury and is a significant vote of confidence in the Swindon and Wiltshire area and the UK. Dyson already employs 3,500 people in the UK, half of whom are scientists and engineers.

Swindon and Wiltshire has a range of education and skills facilities to support the expansion of the advanced engineering sector, including: the Defence School of Electronic and Mechanical Engineering at Lyneham; QinetiQ Apprentice Training School at Boscombe Down; the Empire Test Pilots School also at Boscombe Down and apprenticeship opportunities at DSTL at Porton.

The combination of these assets and their supply chains lays a firm foundation for additional skills development in defence engineering and aerospace across central southern England. This will require teaching and research work across a range of colleges and universities and will support other private sector businesses operating in the advanced manufacturing and aerospace sectors. In the future, these assets will be enhanced by the co-location of defence and public-private defence-related activity as an unique feature of Swindon and Wiltshire, which has the potential to transform not only the local economy but that of neighbouring areas, linking activity in Swindon and Wiltshire with Bristol and Bournemouth and beyond. However, the advanced engineering workforce at higher levels is mobile. This means that the challenge to any area with this type of sector clustering is to cultivate home grown talent to deliver the technical and higher level skills needed to support accelerated developments in this field.

AUTONOMOUS UNMANNED VEHICLES

The development of autonomous vehicles technologies has the potential to revolutionise logistics and distribution, from the use of drones through to innovation in agri-tech and energy applications. Defence industry-related activity in this area will be the catalyst for growth and new technology development in this field in Swindon and Wiltshire and relates well to the foci of the Industrial Strategy Challenge Fund. The opportunity is there to transform the technology of military drones into commercial and public sector applications.

Defence Technology

The defence industry has led much of the development of unmanned autonomous vehicles on land, sea and in the air. Growth of technological developments and applications are continuing to expand at a rapid rate. IHS Markit, a business providing critical information, analytics and solutions for the major industries and markets that drive economies worldwide, commented in January 2017 that over the next 10 years sales of unmanned military aerial vehicles would exceed $82 billion globally, involving 63,000 new vehicles. Many of the unmanned ground vehicles, such as those used in combatting the threat of improvised explosive devices, were delivered more than a decade ago. The IHS forecast is for sales of circa 30,000 vehicles up to 2025, largely to replace existing stock with technologically more advanced applications. Between 2016 and 2025, approximately $4.9 billion will be spent on unmanned ground vehicles globally. Unmanned sea vehicles have been used for decades for mine hunting and exploration, but are still at a relatively early stage of development. The growth in sales for unmanned sea vehicles will be $900m by 2025, compared to the growth of $800m for unmanned ground vehicles. Globally, sales of unmanned sea vehicles will reach $6.5 billion by 2025. The overall market for military unmanned vehicles is huge and growing, accounting for sales close to $100 billion over the next decade.

Figure 1 – Military Drone

Commercial development

Albeit at a much earlier stage of development and with a smaller market, we are beginning to see applications of drone technology within the private and public sector. Dorset Police recently announced the creation of a high-tech drone unit and in so doing are amongst the first police forces to deploy such technology through a dedicated unit. Through collaborative research, the forces across Dorset, Devon and Cornwall began exploring drone use in November 2015. The drones will be used in missing person searches and crime scene photography as well as major traffic collisions. They will also track along the 600 miles of the Dorset coastline to help combat wildlife crime. They will provide operational support across Dorset, Devon and Cornwall. Drones can reach sites of emergencies quicker than road vehicles and are already operating to send aerial video to emergency planning teams. Delivery of first aid equipment and drugs by drones will also enhance survival chances of victims of emergencies.

Private use of drones has caused a lot of concern due to irresponsible and highly dangerous flying of drones near airports and in planes' flight paths. The government's intention to introduce licensing of drone flying is welcomed. Thankfully, there are already businesses that have taken a responsible route to exploitation of drone technology and are registered with the Civil Aviation Authority. Commercial aerial photography is an obvious development, from initial military use to spy on forces and activity from a safe height and in a largely undetectable unmanned vehicle. It provides a cheaper alternative to photography from fixed-wing aircraft or helicopters, whose technology also emerged from military use. For example, in the earlier example of Dorset police's use of drones, they are deploying unmanned vehicles costing in the region of £1,300 to £2,000. Thermal cameras for drone application cost £6,000 and a zoom camera £800. Helicopters cost the Police about £800 per hour. The numbers do add up for drone use and the equipment costs will only reduce as deployment increases.

Drones enable a range of applications as the size and manoeuvrability of the vehicle enable it to get close in and take detailed pictures of small features. This capability lends itself well to inspections of buildings and surveying of sites. It is also a boon to people looking for dramatic views to market products, ideas or to see the impact of a large infrastructure improvement such as a major road or rail-bridge or the regeneration of a city centre site.

Drone technology is also helping to open up the world of planning and development of new and heritage buildings. Using the ability of cameras on drones and application software to render levels of accuracy to millimetres, potential clients and members of the public can see what a building looks like now in its current setting, what the views are like from the building and how light and shadow play out during a day. The new design can be incorporated into the aerial photography to show the proposed updated arrangement and what will change and what will remain the same. Most people find it difficult to translate a two dimensional drawing into a three-dimensional view in their mind. We can already translate a drawing into a three dimensional image on a computer screen and with high-resolution, it is already a much improved product. The merging with actual aerial photography takes the proposition further. It has the great potential to make better informed decisions about building design and planning decisions and can really make public consultation worthwhile and widely accessible.

Figure 2 – Commercial Drone

Use in Agriculture

There is exciting research being carried out by Harpur Adams University, in collaboration with Precision Decision Ltd, into an alternative approach to robot farming. They have called the project the *"Hands Free Hectare"*[11]. The aim is to carry out a full farming cycle from preparation of the land, planting, maintenance and harvesting without any human setting foot on the field. The site will be developed by unmanned ground vehicles and overflying drones controlled by humans using application software. It is the case that a modern farm tractor can already use GPS to decide where, for example, to deposit pesticides and fertilisers and how much in each case. Making the tractors fully autonomous is the next logical step. However, the Harpur Adams study is looking at this issue from a different viewpoint. Existing tractors are heavy, which means they can crush and compact the soil, which reduces yield and their size limits their accuracy when spraying the expensive chemicals. The Harpur Adams team is using prototypes of smaller, lighter and cheaper vehicles which will leave

11. BBC News Report 13 December 2016

the soil in good condition and can deploy chemicals with pinpoint accuracy. The debate is yet to be decided as to whether farming in the future will be dominated by a few large, self-driving tractors or a fleet of smaller robot machines. It is likely the decision will be different on the plains of the USA and East Anglia in this country compared with more compact farms elsewhere in the UK.

Elsewhere in the world, developments march on – with minimum human intervention. Wine makers, despite their industry's reputation for tradition, have been using drones for years to inspect crops and assess the health of the soil. Now, as is often the case, the existence of a problem has created a novel solution. In Burgundy, the shortage of labour to work the vines led to the invention by Christophe Millot of a four wheel vine trimming robot, which learns as it goes and powered by solar panels can operate for between 10 and 12 hours without a charge. In Japan, by 2018, there will be a farm producing 30,000 lettuces a day, which after seeding, have been entirely tended by robots. The impact on workforces is profound. The International Labour Organization estimates that between 1950 and 2010, the proportion of agricultural labourers as a percentage of the workforce declined from 35% to 4.2%. The application of unmanned vehicles will speed up this reduction, with the sector requiring fewer, but more highly skilled, operators.

The commercial reason for this interest in the market for unmanned agricultural vehicles is one of the most developed outside the military. One report, by US firm WinterGreen Research, forecasts that the market will grow from $817m in 2013 to $16.3bn by 2020. But investment bank Goldman Sachs is far more bullish, predicting a $240bn market over the next five years. Manufacturers including John Deere, CNH Industrial and AGCO are all fighting to corner the market in driverless tractors. This places the budget in the agricultural sector on unmanned autonomous vehicles at more than twice the level of the military.

Ploughshare
The story of transforming defence technology into commercial business enterprises would not be complete without a mention of Ploughshare. This business was established in 2005 as DSTL's Technology Transfer Office to actively pursue the commercialisation of publicly funded research for the benefit of all, whilst supporting DSTL's obligations to the MOD. It does this through a mixture of licence agreements and the establishment of spin-out companies. The process of releasing the economic potential of public sector research establishments is often complex and lengthy with a high degree of uncertainty. The research at places like DSTL may be at quite a fundamental level and many steps away from commercial exploitation. Despite these difficulties,

since its inception, Ploughshare has commercialised more than 120 technologies and launched twelve spin-out companies, principally for civilian applications. It anticipates that by 2018, its licence agreements will have created more than 500 high-value jobs, generated exports to the value of £223m and attracted £130m of external investment.

We are now seeing the civilian benefits of years of military research and development. Markets are now well established and surpassing known military spend and economics drives further innovation. We are witnessing cross-over and integration of systems as different sector specialists share ideas and learn from each other. The UK is in a position to consign to the dustbin the oft-used adage that we are not good at converting research into commercial applications. From defence technologies, business enterprises are thriving.

4.5

BUSINESS GROWTH THROUGH INDUSTRY-ACADEMIA INTERACTIONS

Dr. Brian More, Coventry University

INTRODUCTION

I have spent over 40 years working in first industry then academia on business collaborations and partnerships. I now relish the opportunity to dispel some long ingrained prejudices and look to evidence how both sectors are increasingly driven by economic, social and political pressures to engage more for the benefit of society at large. In the United Kingdom universities are seen as essential pillars in the communities in which they reside, offering services not witnessed before as they strive to provide a central focus for society.

Many are classified as large businesses with turnover exceeding £500 million, and provide far more services than just teaching and research to businesses, charities and Government organisations. Universities are seen not only as a source of young talent for business but a cost effective way of industry improving both products and services, discovering new technologies and building upon the skill base of employees. Government sees the universities as prime locations for funding to develop new products and deliver business services to industry. From a theoretical collaborative business model to delivery of tangible results the Triple Helix[12] of Government/Academia/Industry interaction is starting to deliver impact for many countries, a reassuring fact as we enter the Brexit and Trump eras with more uncertainty and risk for international trade.

Industry-academia- interactions are naturally two way; companies of all sizes and legal structures can support the Government's research and education agenda by providing more industry and societal challenges to drive relevant and focussed research. As the skills needs of new business sectors change, the academic base has to be responsive to provide these skills at the right level and right time for global growth in international markets.

Industry has to compete in the global marketplace as international political changes since 2016 have simultaneously opened up opportunities and closed doors to trade and commerce. As UK Government focus shifts towards scale-up business support to grow our economy, no matter what the size of the industry or the state and stage of their development, a collaborative approach to working with academia is recommended.

Internationally developed economies approach industry-academia interactions in essentially the same way, with the trade-off between freedom of publication and intellectual property lock-up the most cited area of conflict[13]. Out of Canada, Japan, the UK and USA only Japan permits companies to control exclusively most collaborative inventions and to censor academic publications. Even in this situation companies are reported as not developing university discoveries to their full potential.

This is a practical chapter aimed to articulate current industry-academia interactions, and offer some guidance as to benefits and challenges going forward.

INDUSTRY-ACADEMIA INTERACTIONS MAKE A DIFFERENCE

One of the latest and most influential reports on the evidence underpinning industry-academia research collaborations is the 2015 Dowling Report[14] issued by the UK Government. Both qualitative and quantitative evidence demonstrate why it is important for both sectors to collaborate to improve their respective businesses. Ideas and

---

12. https://triplehelix.stanford.edu/3helix_concept
13. Industry-University Collaborations in Canada, Japan, the UK and USA –With Emphasis on Publication Freedom and Managing the Intellectual Property Lock-up Problem
14. The Dowling Review of Business-University Business Collaborations, 2015, www.bis.gov.uk

creativity from both industry and academia, and more importantly the multidisciplinary collaboration between both, create new products, processes, services and business models. Early pre-competitive research and an open innovation approach involving many companies and universities has proven to increase innovation through sharing of research results, for example the Structural Genomics Consortium[15].

In the Dowling Report the UK Government recognises the importance of their role in providing strategic leadership and financial support to collaborations in order to drive economic growth. For every pound spent by Innovate UK on collaborative research the Gross Value Added (GVA) was £9.67 where there were 2 or more academic partners, compared to £4.22 without academic partners. Businesses who invest more in R&D are on average 13% more productive than those with no R&D spend; these innovative businesses also see additional benefits in that they are more likely to:

- Be active exporters and achieve better value added per employee;
- Exhibit faster growth – it has been estimated that 51% of labour productivity growth between 2000 and 2008 could be attributed to innovation; and
- As collaborators, produce higher quality research outputs than research conducted either within an individual firm, or on an academic basis alone.

Conversely, for academic researchers the benefits reported included the following:

- Gaining real industry problems to solve, automatic relevance of research;
- Benefiting from working with other disciplines on industry projects;
- Increasing the breadth and reach of funding opportunities;
- Making a positive difference to society, providing their work with meaning and purpose to make a positive difference;
- Accessing new networks;
- Witnessing laboratory research go to industrial scale;
- Seeing new technologies reach the marketplace; and
- Seeing societal impact from academic research– theory to practice.

---

15. The Structural genomics Consortium, http://www.thesgc.org

WAYS OF INTERACTING WITH INDUSTRY

One of the major barriers reported by industry in engaging with universities was the lack of a clear entry point to start the dialogue, and no clarity of the potential benefits. These 2 issues have been overcome by most UK universities with dedicated business facing support teams, with an associated contact website. Figure 1. Shows Coventry University's contact details shown on social media.

Figure 1. Coventry University's Twitter Cover Image

Source: Coventry University, Enterprise & Innovation

Before industry collaborates with a university the following points, taken from the Dowling Report, are considered to be important in achieving success, for all parties concerned.

- Strong and trusting personal relationships;
- Shared vision, goals and objectives defined, setting in place clear expectations;
- Mutual understanding between partners;
- Ability of, and opportunities for, staff to work across institutional boundaries;
- Collaboration brings about mutual benefits;
- Available funding;
- Processes for agreeing contracts and IP are in place;
- Clear and effective communication between partners;
- Organisational support, including senior management buy-in and championing of projects; and
- Willingness from both parties to devote time and resources.

These points for success are mirrored in the USA[16] with additional emphasis placed upon:

16. How Academic Institutions Partner with Private Industry, https://www.rdmag. com/article/2015/04/how-academic-institutions-partner-private-industry

- Identification of leaders who are capable of crossing boundaries between business and academia to foster strong ties; and
- Investment in long-term relationships. A long-term relationship allows parties to share risk and accountability without overburdening a single entity. Under a shared vision and a foundation of mutual trust, a long-term partnership can reap great results by building a body of work over time.

Most industry-academia engagements start with a single project whereby both parties gain trust. If this interaction meets both parties' expectations of outcomes then multiple projects lead to larger collaborative research, strategic partnerships and other large scale projects. For strategic partnerships, universities and industry partners will employ a dedicated client manager to deal with all interactions or touch points between partners.

For practical purposes interactions fall within 10 distinct but not mutually exclusive categories as below:

Collaborative projects and partnerships

In collaborative projects and partnerships, costs are usually shared between parties because each will benefit from the collaboration, e.g. developing a new product, process or service for the industrial partner based upon applied research. Once the intellectual property has been protected by the industry or academic partner, then publications disseminate the results as widely as possible. Often the industry costs are subsidised by Government grants and/or academic partner contributions. In addition to publications, depending upon the collaboration contract, the academic partner may receive an on-going royalty payment through a commercial licence for product sales.

Contract research

In cases where the industrial partner needs to own and control the use of intellectual property from the academic partner then contract research is used. Industry generally will be expected to pay the full economic costs for the research, and their expectation is that the contract will be professionally managed and delivered to industry standards of time and quality.

Continuing Professional Development (CPD)

Continuing Professional Development (CPD) of staff is a key differentiator for industry in growing and competing in the commercial world. Universities deliver accredited CPD courses in most industrially relevant subjects from law, engineering, sciences, leadership, languages and management. Courses are delivered in all the required media formats and locations to meet industry needs – at the university, at the industrial site, at residential locations and, more frequently, on-line. CPD courses and seminars are also delivered by industry, providing an opportunity for academic staff to maintain and build on their knowledge and skills. CPD courses are an excellent way of staff networking and for building lasting relationships on both sides. In addition to CPD, industry/academic staff secondments are a very popular way to build partnerships and expose staff to respective working environments, processes, procedures and priorities.

Expert Consultancy, practical problem solving

Expert consultancy is where industry wants to access the expertise of certain academics when they have an urgent problem which needs solving, in the short term rather than through long or medium term research. The consultancy contracts would be expected to be paid for in full by the industry requesting the service. Examples here might be engineering expertise when a process line fails, or for expert witnesses in court cases. Academic consultants are also used widely for business advice and in the medical sector.

Business space and conferencing facilities

Larger universities run incubator, accelerator and co-working spaces for businesses to locate, work and access academic expertise. These science or technology parks provide both laboratory and office space for spin-out and spin-in companies, often accompanied by large conference centres and meeting rooms. Science and technology parks are also run by industry and will have a specific sector focus, often dictated by the anchor industry, for example pharmaceutical companies (Cambridge BioPharma Cluster[17]), environmental (Hong Kong Science Park[18]), or digital industry (Stanford Research Park, California[19]). Clustering businesses in a sector on a science park, located at or near a university or universities, is a well-documented method of creating value in cities and regions. Running a shared science park with academia and industry co-located creates a hotbed of ideas from cross-disciplinary contacts.

---

17. Bidwells Cambridge BioPharma Cluster, http://www.bidwells.co.uk/assets/Uploads/downloads/biopharma-clusters/research-biopharma-cluster-cambridge-report-rebrand.pdf
18. Hong Kong Science and Technology Park, https://www.hkstp.org/hkstp_web/en/what-we-do/innovation-for-a-brighter-future/clusters-in-focus/Green%20Technology
19. Stanford Research Park, www.stanfordresearchpark.com/

Access to Funding

Hundreds of funding schemes are available for industrial-academic collaborations, particularly in the field of pre-competitive research, for example national (Innovate UK), regional (Northern Powerhouse, Midland Engine), sub-regional (Local Enter-prise Partnerships), European (Horizon 2020, Europe Enterprise Network) and international (Research Councils UK, The Newton Fund, the Industry Engagement Fund). Businesses who collaborate with universities can often use university specialist teams of bid writers who can support them gain access to grants, debt and equity finance. The industry-academia landscape for interactions remains complex (as seen in figure 2 below), so care needs to be taken in using the right scheme for specific desired outcomes.

Figure 2 – Research and Innovation landscape Map (Taken from the Dowling Report 2)

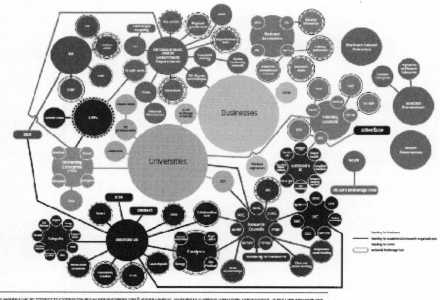

Source: The Dowling Review of Business-University Business Collaborations, 2015, www.bis.gov.uk

Access to intellectual property

Despite opening up the opportunities for both parties for economic growth, IP ownership, use and commercial terms need to be well thought out for both industry and academia when collaborating on projects. This is still the most significant barrier to industry collaborating with academia, and the second most significant barrier for academia collaborating with industry. To help in reaching mutually acceptable terms for IP the Lambert Agreements[20] have been drafted by legal experts in consultation with industry and academia. These agreements have recently been updated and are a good starting point for negotiations, but will require amendments, additions and deletions for each specific contract.

Access to talent, student placements, internships and recruitment

This remains the foundation upon which national industrial growth depends. Many universities have regional schemes to enable easy access to students and staff as part of their commitment to the community. Industry has an important role to play in specifying the sector specific skills and expertise they require. By listening to industry the UK Government and academic institutions have responded to industry need and this has led to degree apprenticeships and more tailored industry specific courses.

Knowledge Transfer partnerships (KTPs)[21]

Knowledge Transfer Partnerships is a UK-wide programme that has been helping businesses for the past 40 years to improve their competitiveness and productivity through the better use of knowledge, technology and skills that reside within the UK Knowledge Base (usually a university).

A Knowledge Transfer Partnership serves to meet a core strategic need and to identify innovative solutions to help that business grow. KTP often delivers significant increased profitability for business partners as a direct result of the partnership through improved quality and operations, increased sales and access to new markets. A KTP Associate is employed by a university partner, but the Associate works full time at the industry partner to transfer their knowledge to the company. A KTP is subsidised by the UK Government and has been widely used by both commercial and non-commercial organisations.

Access to state of the art equipment

State of the art equipment is made available both in industry and academic institutions. Catapult Centres are a recent attempt to drive good research results through technology transfer to market; they were

20. University and Business Collaboration Agreements: The Lambert Toolkit, https://www.gov.uk/guidance/university-and-business-collaboration-agreements-lambert-toolkit
21. Knowledge Transfer Partnerships, http://ktp.innovateuk.org/

set up to support industry in the eight great technologies identified as important to the growth of the UK economy. Similar centres found in Germany are the Fraunhofer-Gesellschaft[22] Institutes.

CONCLUSIONS

Many examples and case studies exist to demonstrate the importance, significance and impact of industry-academia collaborations and partnerships. This includes, for example, the REF Impact Case Studies[23], a collection of 6,975 case studies submitted by UK universities under the research excellence framework in 2014, and the University Industry Innovation Network good practice series 2016[24].

Good partnerships and collaborations can be long lasting and rewarding; many are characterised by committed individuals and champions on both sides. However, challenges tend to arise where the driving force behind the collaboration moves on, where university researchers fail to appreciate the commercial drivers for industrial work or where an industry strategy changes rapidly. Strategic differences for each sector remain; however, the interaction between both is improving as the academic sector employ teams who cross the boundary to specifically grow partnerships.

Today, more than ever, it's time industry started to work closer with the academic base, and universities listen harder to the real world needs of industry to ensure a prosperous and sustainable future.

22. Fraunhofer Institutes and Research Establishments, https://www.fraunhofer.de/en/institutes.html
23. REF Impact Case Studies, 2014, http://www.hefce.ac.uk/rsrch/refimpact/
24. University Industry Innovation Network, Good Practice Guide 2016 Series: Fostering University-Industry relationships, Entrepreneurial Universities and Collaborative Innovation. ISBN 978-94-91901-19-5

CONTRIBUTORS' CONTACTS

Basck
Christian Bunke
Tel. +44 (0) 1223 654547
Email: christian@basck.com

Bosideon Consulting Ltd
Charlie Wilson
Tel. +44 (0) 7880 654113
Email: cwilson@bosideon.co.uk

Brunel University London
Ian Ferris
Tel. +44 (0) 7968 448 332
Email: Ian.ferris@brunel.ac.uk

CIPA – Chartered Institute of Patent Attorneys
Neil Lampert
Tel. +44 (0) 7405 9450
Email: Neil@cipa.org.uk

Coventry University
Dr. Brian More
Tel. +44 (0) 7974 984 928
email: BMore@cueltd.coventry.ac.uk

Creation IP Limited
John Collins
Tel: +44 (0) 141 585 6472
Email: jcollins@creationip.com

Equipped 4 (IP) Limited
Dominic Schiller
Tel. +44 (0) 151 601 9477
Email: ds@equipped4.com

Harwell Science & Innovation Campus
Dr. Barbara Ghinelli
Tel. +44 (0) 7500 106641
Email: Barbara.ghinelli@stfc.ac.uk

Hunters
Gregor Kleinknecht
Tel. +44 (0) 207 412 5122
Email: gjk@hunters-solicitors.co.uk

Imperial Innovations Limited
Jeremy Holmes
Tel. +44 (0) 203 053 8827
Email: jeremy.holmes@imperialinnovations.co.uk

Impetus
Leah Grant
Tel: +44 (0) 1822 819711
Email: leah.grant@impetusip.com

Innovation Birmingham
Cliff Dennett
Tel. +44 (0) 7968 538 989
Email: cliffd@innovationbham.com

J & B Partners Ltd
Steven Johnson
Tel. +44 (0) 7789 908 470
Email: sjohnson@jandbpartners.com

Legend Business Books Ltd
Jonathan Reuvid
Tel. +44 (0) 1295 738 070
Email: jonathan.reuvid@iprevents.uk

May Figures Ltd
Dr. Mark Graves
Tel. +44 (0) 1727 751 080

Julia May
Tel. +44 (0) 1727 751 080
Email: julia@mayfigures.co.uk

Miller Insurance Services LLP
Melanie Mode
Tel. +44 (0) 207 031 2313
Email: melanie.mode@miller-insurance.com

Murray International Partners
Michael Murray
Tel. +44 (0) 7557 805 935
Email: michael.murray@murrayinternationalpartners.com

patentgate GmbH
Margit Hoehne
Tel: +49 (0) 3677 205 9960
Email: mh@patentgate.de

RandDTax
Terry Toms
Tel. +44(0) 1483 808 301
Email: terrytoms@randdtax.co.uk

Sussex Innovation
Mike Herd
Tel. +44 (0) 1273 704 400
Email: mike@sinc.co.uk

Swindon and Wiltshire Local Enterprise Partnership
Paddy Bradley
Tel. +44 (0) 1225 713205
Email: Paddy.Bradley@swlep.co.uk

Taylor Wessing LLP
Graham Samuel-Gibbon
Tel. +44 (0) 207 300 4916
Email: g.samuel-gibbon@taylorwessing.com

Whitespace
Karren Brooks
Tel. +44 (0) 557 135
Email: karren@bewhitespace.com